Breath of Fatal Air

Cedar Fish Campground Series: Book Two

Leslie,
Enjoy the
fun and
games!

D0920744

Zoey Chase

Pages that
move

Pages That
move
Pittsburgh, PA
www.PagesThatMove.com

Printed in the United States of America

First Edition, 2019

ISBN 978-1-951873-03-5

Cedar Fish Campground Map

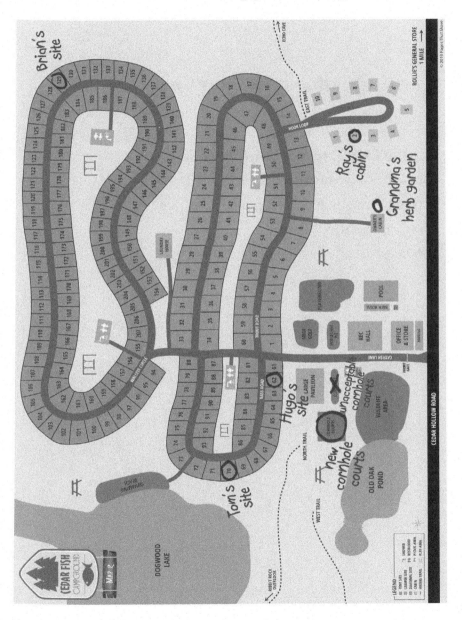

Books by Zoey Chase

Cedar Fish Campground Series
Book 1: Between a Rock and a Deadly Place
Book 1.5: Fishy Beginnings
Book 2: Breath of Fatal Air
Book 3: One Body Short of a Picnic

BREATH OF
FATAL AIR

Find out more about how Gar came to Cedar Fish Campground in the short story "Fishy Beginnings."

When Gar's secret past is discovered, Thea must fight to keep her beloved pet.

Gar, a black Newfoundland puppy, mysteriously showed up at Cedar Fish Campground and became the perfect companion to heal Thea's grief-stricken, dog-loving heart. With such a serendipitous beginning, Thea never questioned the life Gar had before he found her. But one newspaper article could change everything.

Thea discovers a secret about Gar that could mean she loses him forever. With help from her ex-cop security guard, Nolan, and her quirky sidekick, Hennie, Thea must draw on her past to win the right to keep Gar before she loses another treasured pet.

FISHY BEGINNINGS is a short story that takes place after the events of *Between a Rock and a Deadly Place*, book one in the Cedar Fish Campground Series. If you love dogs or have ever lost a pet, you'll love this tale of hilarious animal antics and moments that will both break and warm your pet-loving heart.

Get the story FREE
when you join my mailing list!

ZoeyChase.com/FishyBeginnings

CHAPTER 1

A rumble crept into the stillness of the early morning quiet. A loud muffler. The car making the racket appeared out of the wisps of fog blanketing the road. Gar, my Newfoundland puppy, lifted his head, and I reached down from my seat on the campground's office porch swing to pet him. "This should be interesting," I muttered.

An old silver Dodge Dart, painted with a thick, checkered wave along its body, pulled into the campground entrance. At the back of the car, a bright red and a bright blue corn bag were featured as the dominant art. The front of the car boasted two flags, one on each side like a government official's car, displaying the red, blue, and white logo of the Worldwide Cornhole Organization—the WCO.

Rather than turn into the parking lot, the car stopped in the entrance road, just past the large sign that read "Cedar

Fish Campground." A man in a long-sleeved button-down shirt and sharp pants approached. His tie boasted an image of a cornhole platform and bean bag. I stood and Gar got to his feet beside me. I got a good view of the man's face and froze in shock. A photo jumped into my mind. Grandad, in his late thirties like I was now, sitting on a picnic table, smiling like he was holding back a secret. When I saw the man approaching, it was like that captured image of Grandad had walked out of the photo. I couldn't shake the eerie feeling, and it made my knees wobbly.

"Hello there, fine woman." The man dipped his head and held out a hand to me, palm up. "Hugo Menendez. Who might you be, divine creature?"

I had to remember that this was more than a camper. Hugo was responsible for bringing a huge event to my campground—business I very much wanted to repeat year after year. But he was particular. He'd been hard to work with in the weeks of planning, so I needed to make sure every detail of the event was flawless. That pressure, combined with the bizarre hollow, haunted feeling, made me shaky and scattered.

I blinked at him, then put my hand in his. "Thea Pagoni."

"Exactly who I was looking for and hoped you'd be. That is my vehicle there." He turned to point, as if there were any question. "I don't see your preferred parking, however. Or a valet?"

"Oh, we don't..." I looked around, frantic. Had there been a request for that? Had we missed something?

"No trouble. I'll just leave it there until you've got me checked in."

"We'll get it taken care of right away." I turned and entered the office with Gar.

Hugo was right on my heels and leaned on the counter as I looked up his reservation. "Must be nice living in a place like this," he said. "Quiet and peaceful. You look quite healthy and well rested."

I wasn't sure what to think of the compliment or his tone. Was he... flirting? "Thanks. It's been mostly good."

Hugo pulled a thick book from his messenger bag. "This is the rule book we'll need to go over to make sure everything is up to regulation."

"I've had my handyman working on the things you mentioned in your email."

"Working on?" Hugo straightened up and looked around. "Surely, things are completed and ready for the competition, are they not?"

I gulped. Crap. Were we behind schedule? "Oh, yeah. I just meant... He wants to show you the field and make sure it's all right."

"*Field?* Darling, it's called a *court*." Hugo flipped the book open. "Now, I sent very specific schematics for how the court is to be set up. Surely, your man has read it?"

"Yeah, he..."

I recalled handing the thick book to Nolan, my security guard and campground handyman, shortly after we'd booked the Regional Cornhole Semi-Final Competition. He'd glanced at it, but said he knew how to make a cornhole field. I had trusted him. I'd figured that we had the wooden boxes and corn bags, so what else was there? But now, looking at Hugo's frantic turning of pages, it was clear we'd missed it.

I picked up my new walkie talkie and pressed the button to call Nolan. "Hey, I need you in the office. The cornhole official is here."

"10-4."

I smiled at Hugo. "He's on his way."

Hennie, my friend, sidekick, and honey provider, burst through the door in her muddy galoshes, carrying a large box of various honey products. Her long, silver braid looked frizzy and wild today from the humidity in the June air. "Hey, some jackass is blocking your entrance."

I pressed my lips into a line and widened my eyes at her while nodding subtly toward Hugo.

Hennie set the box down and gave Gar's head a tussle before saying to Hugo, "Well, there. I shoulda guessed that was your car based on all the cornholing." She pointed to his tie.

Hugo turned to raise an eyebrow at her. "And you are?"

Hennie stuck out a hand. "Henrietta Schrute. Proud cornhole fan for a lifetime."

Hugo turned back to me with a smirk. "So glad that some of our fans are as lovely as you."

My cheeks warmed, and I glanced at Hennie, who rocked back on her heels.

I gave her an awkward, sympathetic smile. "Thanks for bringing the order," I said. "You know where to put it."

Nolan stepped into the office. Gar bolted to him, tail wagging so hard that it shook his body. Nolan petted Gar and took Hugo in before approaching.

"Hey there. Nolan Cade." Nolan stuck his hand out and shook Hugo's, hard. "Want to take a look at things?"

"He needs to get to his site first," I said. "So his car isn't in the way."

Hugo waved me off. "It can sit there a while. I need to make sure the courts have been properly designed. It sounds like things have not been up to par around here, and it's very distressing."

Nolan blew out a breath and looked at me.

I gave them both a nervous, apologetic smile. "I'm sure that Nolan will have everything exactly as it needs to be."

Hugo pulled his mouth into another charming grin. "If you tell him what to do, I have no doubt, darling."

I gulped and dared to look at Nolan. His face slid into a glare that mirrored Hennie's. Hugo pushed his way out the door, calling behind him, "Come now, Mr. Cade. Let's get things going as they should be."

Nolan growled in his throat before following Hugo.

"Now, there's a real piece of work," Hennie said.

"Yeah," I agreed, but my stomach tightened. We had to make sure Hugo was happy if this event was going to go well. The way he looked so much like Grandad warmed me to him in a way that played against the repulsion I felt at his smarminess and demanding attitude. Just being in his presence felt like a tug of war on my soul, not helped by the way he'd been over-flattering toward me.

A moment later, my walkie crackled. "Get out here," Nolan said.

Hennie and I hurried out the door, Gar at our feet, as Curtis, my much older employee, shuffled toward us.

"Hey, Curtis." I waved.

He jerked a thumb at the entrance, where his old Buick now sat behind Hugo's Dodge. "Ran out to get milk. Can't get back in."

I said back into the walkie, "We need to get Hugo's car out of the entry."

"*Get over here*," Nolan responded.

Our shoes made squeaking sounds in the wet grass as Hennie and I hurried to the field we'd designated to be the cornhole *court*. We'd had a lot of rain recently, which had softened the ground. I worried it would cause problems. At the court, Hugo's hands were in the air, and he waved his rule book at Nolan.

"Oh, boy," Hennie said, staying close to my side. "This'll be good."

Nolan ran his hand through his dark hair and scowled at me.

"Nothing here meets regulation," Hugo announced. "This is a disaster! My entire career is on the line, you know!"

"Your... career as a cornhole official?" Nolan asked.

Hugo put his hands on his hips. "In two days, we will have twenty-three contestants and hundreds of spectators here for this competition. If it's not perfect, you will hear from my lawyers."

I jumped on that one. "You've already heard from ours." I forced a chuckle. "I happen to be a corporate lawyer." Hopefully that would keep him from making lawsuit threats.

Hugo tilted his head toward me. "Don't you just get better by the minute."

My face flushed and I looked down. Not the response I'd wanted. "It was another life."

"You've got to tell me more about it sometime," Hugo said.

"I hate to break up this little... whatever"—Nolan flicked his hand in the air—"but if we have so much to do, let's get on with it already."

"The courts need to be reconfigured immediately to fix the dimensions." Hugo turned, pointed his nose in the air, and stormed off.

"Where did you find this guy?" Nolan asked me.

I lifted one shoulder and Nolan huffed in response before charging off after Hugo.

I asked Hennie, "Any chance you can help Nolan today?"

She nodded and followed the men.

Another voice called out from the front of the campground, and I looked over to see a chubby man in dress pants and a bright-orange satin shirt hurrying for us, flittering his hands frantically. "Hello! Hello! Help!"

I walked over to meet him. "What can I do for you?"

"There's some sort of backup." He waved toward the campground entrance, where three cars now filled the short space before the gate. "I'm Ray Kline, assistant official. I need to be checked in immediately and taken to my cabin. Hugo Menendez is expecting me."

"You go on then." I pointed in Hugo's direction. "I wouldn't keep him waiting if I were you."

"Oh no, certainly not." Ray hurried off, stepping daintily over the grass.

I went into the office to get Ray's cabin key and check-in form. I'd have to get him to complete it later. I walked outside to inspect the line of cars. Sally, my final employee to arrive at work, sat in her white minivan in the main road, her turn signal on, waiting to turn in. She must not have noticed that no one sat in the three cars ahead of her in line.

Luckily, Hugo had left his keys in his car. For the valet, of course. I hopped in and parked his car in the office lot. I retrieved Curtis's keys from him, then moved his and

Ray's cars as well. Sally turned in behind me and rushed out of her van.

"I am *so* sorry I'm late. I don't know what the holdup was there."

"They left their cars in the entrance," I explained.

"Don't worry about it."

She blinked at me in confusion.

"The officials are already here, and Nolan and Hennie are trying to get things set up. I'll be in to help you at the desk as much as I can. It'll be busy today."

Sally nodded confidently. She took out a small glass vial. "I brought my lavender essential oil, so I'll be nice and calm all day." She grinned and tucked the oil back into her pocket.

Too bad she didn't have her oil last week, when she encountered an older camper who wasn't unhappy, but had a lot of questions and took a lot of time. Sally had been tired and frazzled that morning—her twin boys had had her up late, fighting over who got to sleep with the special blanket. The woman camper had been surprised at Sally's angry outburst, but hadn't held a grudge when I took her aside to explain. The woman must've been a mom, too.

I left Sally in the office, sniffing her oil, and Gar and I returned to the scene at the cornhole court. Nolan and Hennie held stakes and a thin rope while Hugo and Ray held measuring tapes and barked orders over one another.

"Anything I can do to help?" I asked.

Hugo came over to me with an armful of corn bags. "None of these are regulation. I will have to tap into my personal equipment. We'll never get WCO approved bags in time. I cannot believe this—is happening."

"There are regulation corn bags?" I asked.

"Well, of course," Ray snapped.

Gar gave a warning rumble from his chest and pressed his body against me in defense.

"How dare you speak to a woman like that?" Hugo said to Ray. Then to me, "Darling, I know you don't understand the rules of cornhole—it is a rather complicated sport, after all. I'd love to sit down over dinner and explain all the regulations I'm responsible for." He adjusted his armload of corn bags and pulled his mouth into a sneering smile.

I had to look away. When he talked to me like that and looked at me like that—while he resembled my grandad so much—it made my skin crawl.

"Let's get these courts set before you worry about your dinner plans," Nolan said.

Hugo wiggled his eyebrows at me. "It would be my honor to spend the evening with you rather than this imbecile." He jerked a thumb at Ray. "I'm sure you can understand my preference."

I didn't know how to respond. If I turned him down, it might upset him and make him even more difficult to deal with, which would be bad for everyone. But going out with him would be very bad for me. I caught Nolan's disgusted glare and decided to be safe and sidestep. "What's the problem with the courts, exactly?"

"The pitcher boxes are the wrong sizes and the foul lines are off," Nolan snapped. "And the platforms aren't made of thick enough wood and don't have the right paint." I sucked in a breath. "Give me a list and I'll get whatever we need."

Nolan scribbled down a list of items, then thrust the paper at me. "Be fast."

I took Gar with me so he wouldn't be in the way and went to Rollie's, the general store a mile down the road.

I left Gar in the car and hurried inside, making a small jump over the golden lab, Sunny Boy, sleeping in front of the door.

I looked around, but didn't see Enid, the store's owner.

"Thea, dear!" she called out to me.

I turned again as she appeared from the backroom. Today her long cardigan sweater was an outdoor scene. A baby blue sky with a bottom hem of green grass. Three dimensional clouds dotted the sky, and several flowers sprung up from the grass. It was a sweater my grandma would have adored.

"I have to make it fast," I told her as I pulled the list from my jeans' pocket. "Do you have any of these things?" I handed her the list.

She looked it over, shook her head, and handed it back. "Afraid not, dear."

I sighed. "Thanks. This cornhole thing is already a nightmare."

"I got my tickets!" She patted the pocket of her sweater. "I just love cornhole. You know, every year, Rollie and I would have a summer-long competition with your grandparents. Of course, Bettie and Jack always beat us."

"They did live near the cornhole courts. I bet they snuck in late-night practices all the time."

"Well, I never was that good at sports." She shrugged. "I better get going before Nolan strangles Hugo."

I hugged her goodbye before bolting out the door.

I continued on the long trek into the main town of Branson, Missouri. The drive took over thirty minutes, and I had received four new text messages before I arrived, listing more items that Nolan needed to make things right for the competition.

I hurried through the building-supply store and sped all the way back, taking phone calls as I could to alleviate some of the chaos happening in the campground. When I returned in the early afternoon, it appeared as if a global disaster had broken out and hundreds of people had come to Cedar Fish Campground for refuge.

Cars, campers, and people spilled into every inch of the grounds. Inside the office, Sally struggled with the line while Curtis inched his way through the store aisles, helping people find things and answering questions. Nolan and Hennie were still with Hugo and Ray, but now more men had joined the gathering. One group stood directing the other.

Before I could talk to Nolan to get an update, Sally called on the walkie. "Umm, hello? Is anyone there? I need Thea?"

"You don't have to say hello every time, Sally. You can just start talking," I explained. Again.

"Sorry. I think there's a problem?"

"With?"

"Dill. The cat?"

"What's wrong with her?"

The last few weeks Dill had seemed slower and had slept more. I planned to take her to the vet if she quit eating, but that was the one thing she'd been doing just fine. Now, I felt the worry in the pit of my stomach again.

"I'm not sure. She's under your desk and she's panting and meowing funny."

"I'll be right there." I caught Hennie's eye from a distance and motioned for her to walk over. "Can you come with me a minute? Sally said something is wrong with Dill. You'll know better than me."

"Anything to get me away from these creeps," she said under her breath.

Gar bounded along with us. We found Sally in the back office, crying as she petted Dill. A long line of campers waited unhappily.

"Thanks, Sally. We'll take care of Dill if you can just help these campers, please?"

Sally nodded and wiped her eyes before returning to the front counter.

Hennie and I squatted down under the folding table I used as a desk and she looked Dill over. The tortoise-shell cat lay on her side, breathing fast and heavy, and let out a pained mew.

Hennie chuckled and tickled Dill's chin. "Old, rascally girl. Who knew you still had it? Oh, she's fine."

"She is?"

"I'd say within the next few hours, she'll be feeling much better."

"Why is—?"

Then Dill started to lick her back end fervently.

"I'd say she'll give birth within a few hours," Hennie said.

"Should I move her to my cabin?"

Hennie shook her head. "Better not disturb her like that. We'll close the door to give her privacy and she'll do just fine."

I put my hand to my forehead and reached for the travel mug of ice I'd left by my laptop that morning. "Any chance you want some kittens?"

"You've seen my menagerie. I'm not adding to that chaos."

Nolan crackled over the walkie, "I need help up here. What are you doing?"

"Checking on Dill. She's about to give birth."

There was a pause and then, "But she's not giving birth right now?"

"Nope, we're on our way. And we can add 'Find homes for kittens' to our task list because there's no way I'm having a litter running around this place."

"Fine. We have plenty of time to worry about that. Now get over here and get this moron off my back."

CHAPTER 2

The morning before the big Regional Cornhole Semi-Final Competition, I turned the key in the office door to unlock it and found that the anarchy of the day had already begun.

Gar was instantly on alert. Red-brown splotches covered the floor from the office side to the store side. Frantic meowing came from under my desk, not covering the distinctive squeaking of fresh kittens. Dill hadn't only battled giving birth through the night, she'd also had a deadly visitor.

Ricky looked up at me with round, innocent eyes. He held a pretzel in his raccoon paws. He took a bite, and when I lunged for him, he dashed away, hopping into a basket of outdoor toys. Gar barked and chased him. Ricky had likely been in the store for hours, judging by the number of food packages torn open. He'd even smashed a jar of honey by knocking it from the shelf and had helped himself to Hennie's prized product. And then he'd left sticky paw prints all over the aisle.

I chased him outside, then tended to Dill. She lay in a pile of towels, her three kittens nursing at her side. She panted and hissed when I first appeared, obviously on edge from Ricky's presence. She'd probably had to fend him off through the night to protect her babies. I petted her head and got her calmed down, keeping Gar back so he wouldn't upset her again.

"That crazy raccoon is all gone, girl. You just relax."

I cleaned up the blood and Ricky's destruction before the first camper walked in the door, and it wasn't long before I heard the walkie crackle.

Nolan, sounding rather grumpy, said, "You better have coffee because this idiot woke me up an hour ago to discuss the scoreboard."

"On it."

I had my own coffee, but none to share, so Gar and I dashed back to my cabin to put more on. I gulped my existing mugful and poured myself a fresh cup, then filled an extra travel mug for Nolan. I really needed to get a coffeemaker for my office.

I ventured out to the cornhole courts. Gar bolted ahead to sniff all the new things, from the platforms to the rope lines. When I neared him, Nolan looked up from his clipboard.

"Oh, good." He took the mug and sucked in a steaming sip. "Hugo is in the bathroom, so I have a few minutes of peace."

"We have three kittens. And Ricky broke into the store again."

"How does he keep getting in?" Nolan glared toward the office. "You name the kittens yet?"

"Yup. A, B, and C."

He let out a laugh. "Charming."

"They're not staying. They don't need names."

"Don't you think Dill will have an issue with that?"

"She's never kept a litter before. I didn't even think there was a male around for her to mate with."

"There's always a male around when a female goes into heat." Nolan took a long draw from his mug, then showed me the clipboard. "Today's focus is on the practice runs and qualifiers," Nolan said. "At least, that's Hugo's focus, which I guess means it's now mine."

"Sorry. I had no idea it would be so serious and he was going to be so..."

"Uh huh. How was your dinner date last night?"

I rolled my eyes. "Seriously? I didn't have dinner with him. I was running around like crazy. Poor Sally. I thought she was going to quit on me. And Curtis isn't able to help her much."

Nolan nodded. "Good thing we got Hennie around. Where is she anyhow? At least she doesn't get duped by Hugo's fake charm."

"Oh, but I do?" I quirked an eyebrow at him.

He held his hands up in a shrug. "Hey, if he's what you want—that... *type*, then go for it. Whatever makes you happy."

"Well, thanks, but I never said he's what I want."

"Didn't have to. Oh, speak of the devil."

I followed Nolan's gaze to where Hugo emerged from the public bathroom nearest the court. Even though I knew it was Hugo, for a second, it looked like Grandad walking over. I shook the creepiness off.

Hugo jerked a thumb behind him. "Can something be done about these bathrooms, please? They're just awful."

Nolan growled and marked down "bathrooms" on his clipboard list.

"What can I do to help you?" I asked Nolan.

On the walkie, Sally said, "Hello? Thea? Anyone? I need some help."

Nolan smirked. "Take care of that. I got this."

"You sure?"

Hugo piped up. "Sorry to see you go so soon. You are lovely this morning." He blew me a kiss, and I tried not to let my disgust show.

I held up a hand to wave back, not looking at either of them. Gar realized I was walking away and ran to catch up to me, then circled me several times before I entered the office.

It was something of a relief that the office was so busy that I couldn't step away without subjecting Sally to actual torture. The constant line of people checking in, getting questions answered, and making purchases was rivaled only by the phone that refused to stop ringing. I had everyone from press to spectators to actual campers calling to get details about the big competition and our parking and accommodations.

As the day faded into late afternoon, things slowed. Most campers had arrived and were busy putting up tents and building fires. Those coming for the event had had their worries eased and were at home, resting up before their day of excitement.

With so many people around and Nolan being so busy, I'd kept Gar inside most of the day. The strain on a puppy forced to remain indoors, not allowed to participate in the utter bedlam around him, showed in his eyes. I took him for a short walk so we could both stretch our legs. When his paws hit the grass, he tore around and around in large circles, pouncing on leaves and biting at them.

"What a fabulous creature."

I jumped at Hugo's voice. "Oh yeah, he's a great puppy."

Hugo chuckled. "Oh, I meant you, of course."

My cheeks warmed, and I scratched the back of my head while looking away.

"I was just coming out for an early evening game of cornhole," Hugo said. "Care to join me?"

"Oh... I actually don't know how to play." Nor did I want to spend another minute with him.

"The scoring is simple. We play to 21 points."

Nolan walked around the corner of the rec hall and the relief washed over me.

"So, in order to score a point," Hugo went on, "you make your throw."

I nodded to Hugo and met Nolan's gaze as he neared us. "How's it going?" I asked.

Nolan nodded and said, "Things are settling."

"Good."

"How many points your throw earns depends on where it lands, you see," Hugo said.

"You don't have to get it in the hole?" I asked.

"Heavens, no!"

"Man, do I have some stories from today," Nolan said.

Nolan stood closer to me, and Hugo took a few steps nearer, too. I looked at both of them and nodded, trying to divide my attention so neither would be mad. I hoped Nolan knew how badly I wanted to ditch Hugo to hear all his stories.

"If the bag goes through the hole," Hugo said, "you score three points." He held up three fingers.

"I saw this dad," Nolan said, shaking his head, "filling up a huge beach ball with a hose attached to his car's exhaust."

"If the bag lands on the board and stays," Hugo said, "you score one point."

I nodded again, trying to follow both conversations. "I didn't know you could do that," I said to Nolan.

"It works, but it's not a good idea," Nolan said. "If there's a leak..."

"The tricky part in the scoring is the cancellation," Hugo continued, a little louder.

"What does that mean?" I asked Hugo.

Nolan angled his shoulders toward me, trying to edge Hugo out of the conversation. "I stopped and talked to him about it," Nolan said. "I told him it was dangerous."

Hugo explained, "It means that when the other team or person throws their bags, they could cancel out some of your points."

The cancellation concept confused me. Any form of cornhole I might have played as a kid only counted bags that went in the hole. I never knew we'd made up our own rules. "So, you could earn a point by keeping your bag on the board, then the next team could cancel it and you lose that point?" I asked.

Hugo nodded enthusiastically. "Now you're getting it. See, it's not really so difficult to understand, is it?"

Nolan grunted. "Anyway, the dad didn't seem to care much about the danger, so we should keep an eye on that beach ball. It was huge and green and white."

"Wait, why do we need to watch the ball? If it's already blown up, what's the danger?"

Nolan gave me an incredulous look and held his hands up. "Did you hear nothing I just said?"

I ran back through the conversation, but only recalled him saying it was dangerous and then all the crap about cancelling out cornhole points got in the way. I must've missed it.

"Never mind. You obviously have more important things to worry about." Nolan turned and walked away.

Gar followed him, and I had to call out to get him to come back to me. "I need to be going," I told Hugo. "Thanks for the explanation."

I didn't give him time to respond before walking off. When Gar and I were out of earshot, I called to Nolan on the walkie. "Sorry about that. What were you saying?"

It took a long time for him to answer. "Maybe you better get your head out of Hugo's butt and pay attention to your campground."

Anger flooded my chest. "Excuse me?"

"You heard me. You're so twitterpatted by this jackass that you're not paying attention to what's going on with your campers."

"I worked my butt off all day in that office. It was a madhouse! Sally broke into tears twice, and I had to keep giving her water and letting her take oil breaks."

"Take what? It doesn't matter. You have your priorities, and I have mine. I'll be glad when this competition is over and things can go back to normal."

"Right. So sorry for messing up your peace and quiet with a little work."

He grunted and the walkie went silent.

When Gar and I got home, I closed my cabin door hard behind me and flopped on my new couch. I forced the walkie into its charger and sat with arms crossed, glaring at the dark TV while Gar helped himself to the dog food left in his bowl. The cushions of the sofa felt too stiff and the fabric too scratchy. It probably would feel better once it was broken in, but right at that moment, I missed my grandparents' couch. "Stupid Ricky," I muttered. If he hadn't torn the cushion when he broke in and ransacked my cabin a few weeks ago, I could have kept that piece of my childhood.

What was Nolan's problem, anyway? Did he think I just sat around all day? And hello, wasn't he with Hugo all day, so how could he accuse me of being distracted by him? No. This was simple jealousy. Nolan felt threatened by Hugo and was acting out. I laughed when I realized it. It was so obvious now.

I shook it off, knowing that once Hugo was gone, Nolan would be fine and would go back to being himself. As I walked upstairs to my bedroom with Gar leading the way, I glimpsed the photo of Grandad that Hugo reminded me so much of. I stared at it, forcing my mind to pick up on the little details between Hugo and Grandad, like how Hugo's nose was sharper and Grandad's eyes had more prominent laugh lines. They still looked too much alike for me to be comfortable, so I left the photo and went to bed.

I thought I had set my alarm early enough, but the sound of the walkie talkie woke me rather than my phone's beeping.

"You up?" Nolan asked.

I groaned. He already sounded mad. "No," I muttered back.

"I can't find Hugo. We were supposed to meet a half hour ago."

I yawned. "He's probably still sleeping. Like we all should be."

"I'm not the one who set the meet-up time—he did. There's a lot that has to be done before the competition starts."

"I'm getting up. Give me a few minutes."

Gar sat up from the end of my bed and jumped down, ready to start his day. When I stood to stretch, he circled around me, yipping happily. I knelt to rub his head and give him some affection before heading out the door.

We wandered to the new cornhole courts, where neither Nolan nor Hugo nor any living soul was present at this too-dark hour. I turned on my phone's flashlight app and walked Bass Road toward Hugo's site.

The walkie crackled in my hand. "Thea, where are you?"

"Heading toward Hugo's site. Did you find him?"

"Yes. Get here fast."

"What's wrong now?"

"Depends on how you look at it," he said.

I rubbed my eyes. "I'm too tired for this. What's going on?"

"Hugo's dead."

CHAPTER 3

I jolted to a fully alert state as if I'd shot caffeine into my veins. I broke into a jog, and Gar kept up with me easily. This could not be happening again. The first death in my campground had almost ruined me. I didn't think we could sustain another, especially if it meant losing the business of the competition.

When the campsite came into view, Nolan's silhouette stood at the edge, waiting for me. His arms were crossed, and he looked more angry than anything.

"Take photos fast," he said. "I already called the police. You probably only have fifteen or twenty minutes."

"Photos? Are you sure he's dead?"

"Yes."

I blinked at him in shock. "How is this possible?"

"Some coincidences are unfortunate," he said as if he were referring to a flat tire.

"Unfortunate? It's a little bit worse than that, don't you think? Another death?"

"Another murder."

"No." I shook my head. "We're definitely not doing *that* again. He must've died of natural causes."

"You haven't even seen the body."

If this was another murder, I wanted to collect every detail I could. Last time, the police didn't do such a hot job on the case and didn't even catch the killer in the end, I did. Things were just getting back on track in the campground with our reservations and cash flow. A second death would be bad enough, but I couldn't afford to take the hit of a second murder.

I photographed every inch of the campsite: Hugo's Dodge Dart sitting to the right of his tent, tire tracks and tire tread so I could compare them later, muddy shoe prints outside the tent and inside.

"Those are my shoe prints." Nolan picked up a foot and showed me the bottom of his work boot.

I took a photo of his boot, despite his unamused expression.

Nolan stood beside me, holding back the flap of the tent. "I came looking for him and called out. No answer, so I shined the light over the tent to see if he was sleeping. I saw him in there, and when he didn't respond, I unzipped his tent to haul him out."

"What stopped you?"

He held a hand out toward the body. "Look at him."

I shined my light on the body and felt a wave of nausea. I looked long enough to see that Hugo was sleeping on his side. The visible sections of his skin—his face and one arm below a t-shirt sleeve, were very red. I almost dropped my phone when my light shined over a dead chipmunk. "Eww!"

"You're looking at a dead person, but it's the chipmunk that makes you say, 'Eww'?"

"I didn't expect it." I looked again at the chipmunk lying on its back with its paws in the air. It's face, too, looked red, along with the bottoms of its tiny paws. "Why are they both red?"

"Notice that the mattress is deflated?"

"I do now." I quickly took several photos of the body and the chipmunk on the ground beside the mattress, then turned away. "What does that mean?"

"If you'd been listening earlier instead of flirting with Hugo, you'd know."

I put my hand on my hip. "Are you going to be jealous of a dead man?"

Nolan glared at me and continued. "He died of carbon monoxide poisoning." With a toe, he nudged part of the deflated mattress back. "Look at the holes."

I leaned in and saw several tiny holes in a messy line. The first thing that came to mind was that a thumbtack would be the right size and easy to punch into the mattress. A tack would also make small enough holes that the killer might have hoped they'd be overlooked.

"I don't get it. Someone came in and deflated his air mattress and that killed him?"

"Exactly. Just like I told you yesterday."

I stepped away from the tent and pinched the bridge of my nose. Gar sat patiently, as if sensing this wasn't the time to play.

"Can you put aside your annoyance for five minutes and please explain this to me?" I pleaded.

Nolan stepped out behind me. "I answered a call for a completed suicide one time," he said. "Guy sat in his car in his garage with the motor running. His skin was bright red like that, and the coroner said that was a classic sign of carbon monoxide poisoning. Which doesn't make much sense in this case, except that earlier today, I saw a dad blow up a beach ball with a hose connected to his car's exhaust."

I nodded slowly, recalling the parts of the conversation I hadn't missed. "You told him it was dangerous..."

"Right. Because if the ball got a leak and was in an enclosed area, the exhaust could make someone sick or kill them."

"Oh. I thought it was because the ball would explode or something."

"I explained all this earlier."

"What does the dad and the beach ball have to do with Hugo, though? And what about the chipmunk?"

"The chipmunk must've been in the tent at the time. Think about it. If I saw the dad using car exhaust, other people must have, too. Maybe someone even overheard me warning the guy and decided that was a good way to take Hugo out."

"How do you know Hugo didn't see the guy and blow up his mattress himself? It could be an accident." I narrowed my eyes at Nolan. "The only person we know for sure who saw the dad was you?"

"Lots of people were around. And I know Hugo didn't do it himself because he slept on his mattress the night before."

"So, you think someone got this idea and what? Filled Hugo's air mattress with car exhaust, then poked holes in it to kill him?"

"Bingo."

"Not until Tuesday night in the rec hall."

He rolled his eyes. "It's the only thing that makes sense."

"It's the most ridiculous explanation I've ever heard." I shook my head as my thoughts spun. "Nice knowing you. Hope prison isn't too hard on you."

"What's that supposed to mean?"

"You were a cop. Look at the facts. What are the police going to think? Your footprints are all over the site and in the tent. So are your fingerprints. You made it clear that you couldn't stand the guy. You're the one who found the body and had plenty of access to pull off something like that. You're the only one crazy enough to see a dad blowing up a beach ball and think someone could do the same thing to kill someone. You look incredibly guilty."

My words fell over him one by one. His smirk fell into a cold stare that made me feel uncomfortable.

"Much as I wouldn't have minded it, I didn't kill Hugo."

Something in his words chilled me. The anger rather than worry, the annoyance rather than sympathy. The details at the scene might make him look guilty—my lawyer brain couldn't ignore that—but I hadn't really believed he'd done it. I'd only been upset that he'd been so careless. Until his reaction made way for a creeping doubt to slither around my confidence in him. How well did I really know Nolan?

"Let's hope the cops believe you," I said.

"Hey there! Nolan! Thea!"

We both looked behind us into the dim morning light. Ray walked toward us, waving his fingertips.

"I thought everyone was meeting at the courts," Ray said. "Oh, I am just flustered." He fanned his face with a hand.

"Don't worry," Nolan said. "Hugo won't be mad at anything today."

"We can't be sure about that." Ray flicked his head back and forth and whispered, "Where is he?"

"He's dead," Nolan said.

Ray sucked in a breath and put his hand to his chest. "Be still my heart. Can it be?"

Nolan pointed to the tent. "In there."

Ray took several steps back from the tent. "I'll take your word. Well, that's sad, but there's much to be done."

He clapped his hands together twice. "Who do I need to call first?"

"You can use the phone in the office," I offered, "and I'll post flyers saying the competition is cancelled."

"Cancelled!" Ray gasped. "We can't cancel the Regional Cornhole Semi-Finals. We must find a way to go on, in the midst of our tragedy."

I looked to Nolan for help. "I really don't think that's a good idea. The police will be here soon to investigate the scene."

"While it's terribly sad and unfortunate timing," Ray said, "we can't allow this to derail things. We must have a candidate to send to Nationals."

"Do you really think people will want to stay with a murderer possibly running loose?" I asked.

"Murderer?" Ray's face whitened. "I misunderstood." He took a moment to gather himself.

Another man came toward us, walking fast. "Ray! There you are. What's going on? Where is everyone? We're all waiting."

I checked my watch. The contestants and officials were all due to meet twenty minutes ago for the final check-in.

The man who now stood talking to Ray wore a shirt that said, "Slide it in your cornhole." He held a small corn bag in his hand, rubbing it like a worry stone. He squeezed the bag and tossed it from hand to hand as he spoke.

"We need to stick to the schedule," the man insisted. "Where is Hugo?"

Ray held up a hand. "That's the problem, Brian." He dropped his voice to a scandalous whisper. "He's been murdered."

Brian scrunched up his face. "No. That can't be right."

Ray nodded solemnly and looked to us for confirmation.

"The police will be here any minute," I added.

Brian's eyes widened. "We better stay out of their way. We need to get over to the courts anyhow."

"I don't know if we can..." Ray looked to us again.

"We're going to have to cancel the competition," I said.

"No, we can't! We can't let this stop us!" Brian punched a fist into his hand. "Cornhole won't be tainted by the violence of this world. We're better than that!"

Ray puffed up his chest and nodded once. "What would everyone think if we let one bad egg destroy the entire championship?"

"This is our time to rise up!" Brian pumped a fist into the air.

Ray added, "Cornhole is about more than violence, and we must show the world that we're strong and nothing will stop us." He raised one fist proudly.

My mouth hung open and I looked to Nolan.

He took a moment, then said to me, "Going on with the competition would help keep the media attention from another murder in the world's most dangerous campground."

"It is not dangerous!" I said. "But maybe you're right. The police might be able to gather information without a public panic."

"It would also keep witnesses at the scene," Nolan added. "And we can probably keep the murder quiet more easily. If we cancel a major competition, people will wonder why, and they'll have all day with nothing else to do but figure it out."

I rubbed my forehead. "I can't believe we're doing this."

"The competition will go on!" Ray exclaimed. He and Brian marched off toward the cornhole courts.

"Do you think anyone will be sad that Hugo's gone?" I asked.

"Not a chance," Nolan said.

"Are we really going to do this again? Find clues and suspects, try to solve this thing?"

"We can always leave it to the Outer Branson Police Department."

I shook my head. "That worked out so well last time." If it hadn't been for Nolan, I might be dead because of the PD's incompetence.

"Then I guess we have another murder to solve," he said.

"Great."

"Until then, we have a cornhole competition to run."

CHAPTER 4

I had gone to the front of the campground to wait for the police, since Sally wasn't in yet and Curtis wasn't up and on duty yet.

While I waited, I sent a text to Hennie. "There's been another death. Another murder. Cops will be here soon."

When the police arrived, I directed them to Hugo's site, number 70 on the smaller tent loop. I then walked back to the site, where they had already started photographing and marking off the scene.

Nolan stood talking to Officer Randall—the one who looked like the stereotypical cop-who-ate-too-many-donuts. Randall's beanpole of a partner, Officer Longshore, spotted me and waved me over.

"We have some questions for you," he said.

"I figured you would, but I don't know much."

"You've been interacting with the victim over the last... two days?" He referred to the small notebook in his hand.

"Hugo arrived two days ago, yes. He's been mostly working with Nolan, but I talked to him many times."

"And did he seem okay to you?"

Well, he was creepy and flirty and demanding, so no.

"In what way?"

"Was he agitated or depressed at all?"

"Hugo's usual state seemed to be agitation. He was... difficult. But no, he didn't seem depressed. It wasn't a suicide."

"And you know this for sure?" Longshore paused in his writing to look at me.

"Well, no. But it seemed like a murder based on the scene."

"You inspected the scene? Why did you feel the need to do that? You may have contaminated evidence. That's a serious crime."

"I didn't touch anything." I thought it was better not to mention the part about how I had to see the scene for myself since I couldn't rely on the police to solve the murder.

"You like looking at dead bodies?"

I scrunched my face in disgust. "Definitely not. I'm just being diligent."

Longshore pursed his lips and nodded. "Right. Or you're trying to cover something up. Like, for a friend maybe?"

"There's nothing to cover up."

"Interesting." Longshore tapped the pen against his lips and narrowed his eyes at me. "Don't you think it was a coincidence that Nolan had been angry at Hugo, then found the body, while his physical evidence is all over the crime scene?"

"He's the handyman and security guard. His physical evidence is all over the entire campground, so no, I don't think it's strange. He's been working closely with Hugo, so he was the most likely to find him."

"And also the most likely to kill him."

I raised an eyebrow. "Since when do the police make assumptions and batter witnesses about it?"

He frowned. "I'm not. But we're looking at Nolan, and we need to get all the information we can. We've been told you have cameras?"

"We do, but they don't cover every inch of the campground. Mostly just the front buildings."

"We'll need to take that footage."

And that was exactly why I'd gone with a cloud-based system when I upgraded the cameras after our first murder. When the police took their copy, I'd still have access to the footage from anywhere I could connect to the internet. But they didn't need to know that part.

"I'll be happy to give it to you. Anything else you need?"

He looked back over his notebook. "Where were you at the time of the murder?"

"Well, I'm not sure when it took place, but this morning, I was sleeping in my cabin when Nolan called."

"The victim was last seen alive at 11:15 p.m., according to your employee. And found dead at 5:45 a.m. by the same employee. If he can be believed."

"Last night I was in my cabin." After my little tiff with Nolan. That twisting doubt crept its way back in. I had gone to bed before 11, so Nolan saw Hugo after he talked to me. Could our argument have sent Nolan over the edge? I shook the thought away. He couldn't have done something like this.

"No?" Longshore asked.

"What?"

"You said you were in your cabin, then you shook your head."

"I was in my cabin. The head shaking was unrelated."

"You sure? You weren't maybe with Nolan, helping him kill Hugo?"

"Nope. And Nolan didn't kill Hugo."

"Do you have any proof to back that up?"

"I know it in my gut." The moment I said the words, the doubt burned in my throat, as if it knew I'd lied.

"Who do you think might have done it?"

"Hugo wasn't much liked and there are a ton of people here for the competition. I guess any of them might have done it."

"That's helpful," he said sarcastically.

I cocked my head. "I'm sorry, I thought it was *your* job to investigate the crime, and that you didn't want me to interfere. That's what you all keep telling me, even though I solved the last murder before you did."

"You got lucky last time."

"I wouldn't call what happened lucky, but that doesn't change the fact that it's your job to figure this out, not mine." So, it was looking like this would be on me again to solve. I'd have to find something along the way to clear Nolan, too.

"We will get this thing solved." Longshore didn't even sound like he believed it himself.

"I sure hope you do. Is there anything else? We have a competition to run."

"I see you're not sad about the death at all. That's interesting."

"I care. Someone died in my campground, and that's awful. But I didn't know him, and I have another few hundred campers here and more people on the way to see the players toss their corn bags. If they don't have a competition to watch, they'll get much more interested in what you're doing, so I'd say it's in the best interest of the investigation if you let me and Nolan get to work."

Longshore glanced behind him at Randall, who was still talking to Nolan. "Still interviewing that particular suspect."

"Suspect? On what grounds do you have to make him a suspect?"

Longshore checked his notebook. "Uhh... Person of interest, I mean. Unless Randall got something good."

I sighed. "Am I done?"

"For now." Longshore glared at me as I walked off. I went straight toward the cornhole court, with Gar happily trotting along at my side. He seemed to really enjoy all the extra people around. That many more hands to pet him, dogs to sniff him, and kids to drop food for him to eat up. He was the perfect campground dog.

Hennie's four-wheeler rumbled into view. "What happened? Who died?" She hollered as she pulled up closer.

"Shh!" I looked around to see if anyone overheard. Luckily, no campers were nearby. "Can you not announce it to the world? I'm sure everyone will know soon enough."

She slowed down to my walking pace, driving right beside me, and hissed, "Then tell me who!"

"It was Hugo."

Hennie gasped and her eyes widened. "Well, looky. Sometimes karma does get you."

I shrugged. "Maybe. Nolan is talking to the police. They think he's a suspect. I have to go find Ray and make sure they're all set."

"The competition is still going on, right?"

"Yup." In the distance, I could hear a voice making announcements over a loudspeaker. "I'd say they're starting soon."

"Then I'm off to watch. I'll get details after." Hennie zoomed away and vanished from sight.

When I reached the cornhole court, I found Ray easily in his very red shirt. Was his whole wardrobe satiny short-sleeved button-downs? He had taken over and was proudly running the competition from the sidelines of the court.

"Need anything?" I asked him.

Ray beamed back at me. "I was made for this!"

He scurried off, shouting commands to someone, and I took that to mean he was just fine.

I continued on to the office. Sally would be in by now, and I wanted to make sure she was okay.

The store end of things was slower than it had been, since most people were busy watching the competition. But many came in search of refreshments and hit up our soda machine and ice cream freezer. Now that it was June, keeping ice cream on hand was an absolute must. I planned to reopen the rec hall cafe next season and include soft-serve. Until then, individually wrapped items were all we could offer.

In my office, I sat at my desk and logged into our security system. The tiny kittens slept in their box under my table desk. I petted Dill, checked her food and water, and got to work. Gar sniffed at them, but backed off when Dill hissed, and found a comfortable place to curl up nearby.

There was a huge time span of footage to search: 11:15 p.m. to 5:45 a.m. This was further complicated by the fact that the mattress could have been tampered with earlier in the day. If someone really had filled Hugo's air mattress with car exhaust and poked holes in it to kill him, they couldn't have done all that while Hugo was sleeping on top of the mattress. Because the holes were so small, it could have been hours earlier—it wasn't until Hugo laid on the mattress that enough pressure would have forced the gas through the holes. But the killer also could have filled the mattress with exhaust just minutes before Hugo returned to his site for the night.

So, at almost any point in the day, the killer might have gone into Hugo's tent. I had hours and hours of footage to review. My list of people to question grew speedily with so many campers on the grounds and all of them moving around so much with the pre-competition goings on—photo sessions with the contestants, practice opportunities, autograph booths, merch tables. And that was on top of the campground's everyday amenities like the pool and playground, which were also packed. Nearly every person in the campground could be considered a person of interest who might have seen something at Hugo's campsite that day.

I made a copy of the footage and gave Sally a flash drive for Longshore and Randall. Then I started to watch the camera feeds. I lost track of time and almost jumped out of my skin when Hennie knocked and opened my office door hours later.

"It's halftime." Hennie sat in the other chair, beside me.

I sighed. "I'll be glad when it's over. Do people know what's going on?"

"I don't think so and the police are gone now. What's that?" Hennie pointed to my very long list of people where I'd written at the bottom, "Everyone!"

"My impossible list of people to question."

"You can't question *everyone*."

"I know that. That's what makes it impossible."

"You just solved a murder last month. You should be a pro at this by now." She looked at the list more closely. "I think you're on the right path with that Ray and Brian. But why is Nolan on there?"

"I need to find something to clear him since the police think he's a suspect."

"Start with those three then. Don't stress yourself all out." Hennie bent under the table and went to the box of kittens. She picked up the orange one and thrust it at me. "Hold a kitten. That'll make you feel better."

"It'll make me feel better if I know they have a home to go to when they're weaned." I petted the tiny cat until it started to squeak so pitifully I had to return it to its mother.

"They could be good for business." Hennie held up the grey and white kitten in one hand and the black and white one in the other. "Look how cute."

"They look like blind rats."

"Give them a week or two."

"I'm getting out of this office for a while and going to talk to Nolan. I'm not sure what his official alibi is."

Hennie put the kittens away. "I better get back to it. Don't want to miss a single match."

"Have fun." I picked up my notebook and a pen.

Hennie and I walked out, waving as we parted ways.

I called to Nolan on the walkie. "You around?"

"Taking a break at home."

Gar and I continued on to Nolan's permanent site and found him sitting on his porch, softly playing a classic rock song on his guitar.

"Your cornhole duties are all done?" I asked.

"Nothing else to do once the competition started. I needed a few minutes to hide out."

I sat on the padded chair beside him. "I came to get your official alibi."

"Don't have one." He strummed a few more chords.

"What did you tell the police?"

"Well. At the time of death, I was sleeping after a hard day's work, alone. And during the day, I was all over the place. I could have easily tampered with the mattress."

My eyes widened. "And you told them that?"

"Should I have lied?"

"Well, no, but... You didn't have to point it out, either."

He lifted a shoulder and switched songs. "They'll investigate me."

"And you're not worried about that?"

"I did nothing wrong, so I have nothing to hide."

"Yeah. Good thing no one innocent ever goes to jail."

He put his guitar down. "In that case, let me also point out how much I couldn't stand the guy. In fact, after the two days I had with him, you might even say I hated him. So there was motive on top of all the opportunity I had.

Heck, I even found the body and pointed out the cause of death."

I looked down at my hands. I hated that I didn't know for sure he was innocent. "How are you going to prove you didn't do it?"

"I'm not. They'll figure it out."

"Who do you think did it?"

Nolan huffed. "That idiot? Probably did it to himself, not realizing car exhaust is toxic."

"He poked holes in his own air mattress? Why would he do that?"

"I'm looking at the guy who blew up the beach ball with his car exhaust. You said yourself how strange that was. Tom is the only person I've ever seen do that."

"I wonder if he has a history of violence," I said.

Nolan crossed his arms and smirked. "If you're using that as a qualifier, then you can go back to making me the prime suspect."

I pulled my eyebrows together. "What do you mean?"

"I've killed several people."

Shock burst in my chest. What could I say to that?

"Think about it, Thea," he snapped. "I was a cop for twelve years and a solder for two. Yeah, I've killed people. That's what you do in war. That's what you do when the job calls for it."

I took a moment to let this sink in. I knew he'd been a cop and in the marines, but I hadn't considered whether he'd actually killed before.

"So there," he said. "You convinced now?"

"I'm sure we'll find something to clear you."

"Good luck."

My head and heart warred as I walked back to the office. Nolan was a killer. He'd told me as much. And not only that, but several times over. Certainly, it would be easier to kill again if he'd already committed so much violence in his past, even if those killings weren't murder.

My heart focused on the good things about Nolan. The way he played with Gar and helped me. The way he could fix anything and not much seemed to bother him. The way he'd protected me. But then, he'd also let his temper show when we'd caught the first murderer of Cedar Fish Campground.

Did Nolan really hate Hugo enough to kill him, though? A few days of being annoyed didn't seem like it would push Nolan that far. He'd been jealous as well, but his feelings for me would have to be fairly strong if it led him to kill. And so far, neither Nolan nor I had said much about feelings except that we wanted peace and healing.

I wanted to know all I could about Nolan Cade. I searched for him online and read the results over our slow internet. Not much came up under his name. I found a few social media profiles, but the posts were old. His name was mentioned in a few articles where he'd been involved in bringing down a criminal in his cop days. There was also more than one Nolan Cade in the world. But one article showed his photo from a few years ago.

A few paragraphs from a St. Louis paper claimed Nolan was fired from the police force and that an investigation had been pending. I read it twice, but found nothing to indicate what he was being investigated for. Could murder possibly have been involved?

When I jumped at the sound of the door opening, I realized how tense I was.

"Hey there!" Hennie called out as she let herself into my office. "It's all done. Brian Melton is the champ." She looked me over. "What's your trouble?"

"Nolan."

"Man trouble. Spill." She flopped into the extra seat and reached down to pet the kittens.

"He might have murdered Hugo."

"Still didn't find something to clear him?"

"No, and I don't think I'm going to. Hennie. I think he might have done it. He admitted to me that he's killed multiple people."

She nodded. "I'm not too surprised he has, given his past. But you really think he would kill? Seems like a good guy to me."

"I don't know. I wouldn't have thought so, but things fit. Motive is the thing I'm weakest on. He was mad at Hugo and couldn't stand the guy, but I don't know if that was big enough to kill over."

"Well, you're missing the obvious."

"What's that?"

"He was green as could be with envy! Hugo flirted with you like mad, and for God knows why, Nolan convinced himself you liked him back. Nolan was not happy with Hugo one bit, believe you me. And after the way he treated us for two days? I wanted to strangle him my own self."

I gasped and put my hand to my mouth. "I said that. Days ago. I told Enid that I had to get back before Nolan strangled Hugo."

"It must be in your subconscious as a possibility."

I threw my hands into the air. "You're not helping!"

"I just see that it makes sense, is all. Nolan was all over the scene, violent past, plenty of opportunity, multiple motives. If it weren't Nolan, someone matching that lineup would be our top guy for sure. What are the police saying?"

"He's a suspect." I grabbed my travel mug and chomped a piece of ice. My head wouldn't stop pounding.

Hennie picked up the black and white kitten and stroked it as she thought. "Hmm. Didn't Nolan log into something before to get secret cop information?"

"The police database, using his brother's account. I don't know if he will again, but I can't ask him to do that."

"Why not? He probably wants to know himself."

"I don't want to make him mad."

She quirked an eyebrow at me. "I don't think he'd be mad over that."

I looked up at her and then back down. "I don't know what to think of Nolan right now. How well do I even know him? The thing is..."

Hennie watched me, patiently waiting.

"I thought I knew my ex-husband," I said. "You're married to someone for six years, you think you know what they're capable of. But I was really, really wrong." The words caught in my throat and made my eyes burn. "I thought Nolan was one of the good ones. But he has way more of a past than Russell did, and look how Russell turned on me. He almost killed me, Hennie." The tears welled and overflowed. I wiped them away quickly, but new ones followed.

I hated thinking of my ex and the way our marriage had so violently and dramatically ended. It was the worst night of my life, followed by the worst two years of my life. I'd been too frightened to even consider dating again. Nolan was unexpected, and I'd been careful to keep my feelings under wraps. Now I wondered if I'd let myself go too far too fast. I didn't really know that much about Nolan, and what I did know could be scary. Now, it seemed that my warm feelings toward him weren't letting me see the situation clearly. I didn't know what to think, and that terrified me.

"Oh, honey." Hennie put her arm around my shoulders. "Nolan might be a tough man, but I don't think he'd ever hurt you. And if he tried, you could defend yourself."

My mind flashed to the time Nolan and I had been playing around and I was unable to break free of his grip. He was incredibly strong. "We haven't been practicing enough."

"Then let's get to it." She jumped up and moved into fighting stance.

"I'm too tired for karate. And my stomach hurts." I wiped my eyes again and sniffed.

Hennie gave a sad smile. "You two need to just confess your feelings and be done with it. You wouldn't be tore up like this if you didn't feel something for him."

I shook my head. "You know that can't happen. My feelings are already in the way. And besides, there are no feelings to talk about. There's nothing going on between us."

"Just because you don't want the feelings to be there, doesn't mean they'll go away. No point in lying to yourself. Haven't you done enough pretending?"

I took the grey and white kitten from the box and held it close to my chest. The warmth and fragility of the tiny animal comforted me. "What good would it do now? If he's guilty, he'll be going off to prison."

"Come on, you really think he did it?"

I blinked, and the tears I thought I had under control spilled down my cheeks. I wiped them away. Not that long ago, I would have bet my life on the fact that Russell would never raise a hand to me. If I was wrong once, I could be wrong again. "I don't know what to think. Of course I don't want him to be guilty. But I can't deny the facts, and he's not denying them, either. He says he didn't do it, but nothing proves that."

Hennie took a handkerchief from her pocket and handed it to me. I dabbed my eyes and handed it back.

"I guess you'll have to wait it out and see what the police come up with," she said.

I nodded sadly. "Until then, want to help me try to solve this thing? I've got some people to talk to."

CHAPTER 5

"I think it'll be easy to start with the champion," Hennie said as we left the office. "Perfect excuse."

"Brian Melton it is."

Brian's campsite was the farthest of all those we planned to talk to—site 129 in the outer loop, by the sole black locust tree in the campground. I didn't mind the walk, and neither did Gar as he trotted along between us. Good chance to stretch my muscles and get the blood flowing so I could think through this more clearly.

Brian stood in his campsite talking with two guys when we approached. They snapped a few photos, and the guys walked away a moment later.

"Did you want to get a photo?" Brian grinned, proudly displaying his "Cornhole Champion" t-shirt and the gold medal hanging around his neck.

"Yes, if you wouldn't mind."

"My pleasure." He gave me a leering grin and his gaze drifted below my chin.

I wanted to roll my eyes at him for so obviously checking out my boobs, but I had to play along for long enough to get him talking. I took my phone from my pocket and snapped a few pics.

"Could we ask you a few questions, too?"

"Certainly." Brian kept his grin pasted on his face. He held a corn bag and tossed it gently into the air before catching and tossing it again. "Everyone wants to know more about me today." His eyes, again, drifted to my chest. And stayed there.

"Do you have any pre-competition rituals?" I asked. "What sort of things were you doing the night before the competition?"

"I practiced all night. I wanted to make sure my tosses landed perfectly. See, each platform and each court is a bit different, and it takes time to get to know it."

I nodded as if I cared. "And how about during the day? What did you do the day before the competition?"

"We had the pre-qualifiers, so I was at the courts for that. Between pre-qualifiers and practicing, I had a big dinner of spaghetti to carb load. That wasn't too easy while camping, but I made it work." He pointed proudly to a pot caked with pasta chunks and tomato sauce.

"The pre-qualifiers took several hours," I pointed out. "Did you step away at all to do anything while they were going on?"

Brian thought, then said, "No. I had no reason to leave."

"You and Ray insisted on holding the competition, despite the murder of the head official. Did the crowd seem affected at all by that?"

Brian laughed. "I won't deny that I wasn't sad to see Hugo go, and I haven't found a person yet who is. If anything, I think it made the crowd more excited."

I glanced sideways at Hennie. Her eyes widened slightly. When I looked back at Brian, he was staring at my chest.

"I guess I would have expected at least some sympathy for the dead," I said. "Some respect for the position he held in the cornhole world."

"It is sad when we lose someone high up," Hennie said.

"We had a moment of silence," Brian said defensively.

I shrugged. "I think the way the whole thing went down made a lot of people look guilty of the murder."

Brian frowned. "Like who?"

"Well, you happened to show up at the scene," I said. "Like you knew it had happened. And you pushed Ray to hold the competition, anyway. Seems a little heartless."

Brian huffed and gripped his corn bag tight in his hand. "I was looking for Hugo, that's why I was there! I was concerned about him!"

"I'd say Ray also looks guilty, so it's not just you."

"You think I would harm an official the night before the semi-finals?" Brian's voice neared hysteria. "I would *never* jeopardize my cornhole career like that!" He shook his corn bag at me. "You want to see someone who really hated Hugo, look at Ray. He had the most to gain from Hugo's death!"

"And why's that?"

"Ray told people that he should be the head official. He thinks he did a better job than Hugo. So, there you go. If Hugo's gone, Ray's in. It had to be Ray."

"*Had* to be?" Hennie clarified.

"Do you think Ray is capable of murder?" I asked.

Ray was what my grandad called "soft city folk." He had hunted me down to ask for extra-strength bug spray and had requested that his cabin—especially the shower— be cleaned daily.

"I think people can be pushed to do all sorts of things," Brian said.

His words chilled me. I'd been thinking too much about what people were capable of if they were pushed too hard. Was it possible that Nolan had been pushed beyond his breaking point?

"I think you might be right," I said. I couldn't think of any other questions, so I lifted a hand to wave. "Well, congratulations on your win. Thanks for talking with us."

"Any time." Brian gave that same creepy smile and took one last look at my breasts before I turned away.

When we were out of earshot, Hennie asked, "What do you think?"

"He's strange. And takes his cornhole career very seriously. I'm not sure if it's so seriously he wouldn't risk it or so seriously he would kill for it."

"He's right, though." Hennie stopped to pick up a stick and toss it for Gar to retrieve. "No one at the competition seemed sad that Hugo was dead."

"Can't say I'm too surprised. But that doesn't help us narrow it down."

We walked to the cabin where Ray was staying. When I knocked, he pulled the door open hard an instant later.

"Oh, thank goodness!" He threw his hands up in the air. "It's a horrible infestation!"

"What do you mean?" I glanced at Hennie, who shrugged.

Ray ushered us inside and over to a corner of the main room of the cabin. I could smell fresh, lemony cleaner—a scent we didn't use. When I took a quick glance around, every surface seemed to sparkle. Ray had come to rent a cabin in a campground in the woods and had cleaned it to a spotless finish. Maybe I could hire him when this was all over.

I turned my attention back to where he was frantically pointing, hopping from foot to foot in squeamish disgust. I had to look hard, then I spotted the line of ants climbing down the wall, into the baseboard.

"I called down to the main office hours ago, and no one has been out here to handle this," he complained.

"Oh. I didn't come—"

Hennie walked over and squished the foot of her galoshes against the wall, killing the ants. "There ya go."

Ray let out a shriek of horror, and I gave him an apologetic smile. He dashed to the kitchen to retrieve paper towels and a spray bottle, then sprayed the wall, wiping away the ant carcasses with an expression on his face of utter revulsion.

"We actually came to talk to you," I said.

"Well then, your staff here is not very efficient."

"Sorry. My staff consists of four including me, and it's been busy," I said. "We came to check on you and see how you were feeling."

He fanned himself and sat on the couch. Gar sat near him and Ray reached out to pat his head twice. "Thank you for asking. It's been difficult. I had to run the competition by myself at the last minute, and so much paperwork to do! You wouldn't think someone dying would require so much work! It's exhausting."

"You're not feeling any... grief over losing Hugo?"

Ray let out a long sigh. "I would never wish a soul any ill will, but I didn't like the man very much."

"Someone said you hated him."

"Hate is such a strong, nasty word." He scrunched up his face. "But I guess it does apply in this case. I mean, the man didn't even pay for his education! He went through a free online program to become an official. He shouldn't be legal, if you ask me. We do need to have standards, after all. And now that I've had the chance to run such a major competition, the WCO will see my value as an official."

"Would you say you had the most to gain from Hugo's death?" I asked.

"How should I know? I hardly knew the man."

"What were you doing the day before the competition?" Ray pulled his head back and squinted at me, then Hennie, then back to me. "Are you... questioning me?" His eyes grew and his hands flittered into the air. His words burst out in a rush. "I was very busy the night before, reviewing the rule book. I wanted to make sure I knew all the regulations. I was up late, but in my cabin the whole time."

"Why were you reviewing?" Hennie asked.

I watched his answer carefully. If he'd known the night before that he would be the one officiating, that would indicate pre-meditation and some level of involvement.

"An assistant official has to be ready at any time, for anything. As you can see, you never know when you'll be called on. Think if I hadn't studied. I might've forgotten some rule and blown the whole thing."

"What about during the day?" I asked. "Someone got into Hugo's tent at some point."

"I was with him the whole day! You saw us. We were running around like mad getting things ready."

"And at some point, might you have had time to slip away and get to Hugo's campsite?"

"Well, no, I..." He thought more about it. "Perhaps, but that certainly doesn't prove anything. Anyone could have gotten in there if Hugo was tied up all day."

"Anyone in particular you think might have done it?" I asked.

Ray took a moment, looking relieved to have the pressure shifted from himself. "The winner, Brian Melton? He's always seemed a little funny to me."

Ray thought *Brian* was strange? I almost choked on my laughter, but managed to hold it back. I guess everyone was strange to someone. "How so?"

"Quite intense about getting his way. I happen to be on his good side, but I've seen what happens to those who aren't. Hugo wasn't one for taking bribes, but I've heard Brian is one for giving them. If Hugo turned him down and didn't do what he wanted..."

"Did he bribe you?" I asked.

Ray took on an indignant look and clicked his tongue. "I am a fair and honest official. I wouldn't need to be bribed."

I raised an eyebrow at Hennie. Maybe he didn't understand how bribes worked.

"I wanted to be like him, if you must know," Ray looked off in space and shook his head slowly. "Hugo Menendez was a big name in the cornhole world. I admired him, in some ways. I felt honored to work under him."

A strong hint of insincerity rang in his tone. I doubted we would get anything more out of him. I stood up and Hennie and Gar followed.

"We should be going. Thank you for talking to us," I said.

"You'll make sure someone comes to spray for the infestation?" He looked worriedly at the spot where the ants had been. "I don't want them to come back."

We probably had a can of bug spray somewhere that would appease him. "Sure."

As we walked out, I noticed Ray's car. It was bright white, but what caught my eye was how curvy the body looked. I snapped a pic of the car and its treads.

"What do you make of that?" Hennie jerked her thumb back toward Ray's cabin as we walked off.

"I think he's got enough jealousy for a motive and not much of an alibi."

"Seems no one's got one of those."

"Not a good one, anyway. I just don't know if Ray could have done it. He can barely handle staying in the cabin, let alone connecting a hose to a car's exhaust pipe."

"But if he was gonna kill someone, it would be some kinda highfaluting death like air poisoning. Couldn't see him shooting or strangling or stabbing."

"Definitely not. Imagine the mess of a stabbing!"

Hennie chuckled. "So, now what? That's everyone, isn't it?"

"We need to talk to that dad with the beach ball, Tom Adkins, who Nolan mentioned. Then there's the rest of the campground."

"Let's start with the dad. We're not going to get much further today."

She looked up at the patches of fading light visible between the trees. It had been a long day, and I was feeling it in my bones.

As we walked, I noticed a lot of people packing up. Most of the campground was booked for the competition, but I had a feeling that the police walking around asking people about a possible murder might have sent some folks home early.

At Tom's site, number 62, we found him tending to a campfire while his wife helped a small boy with a juice box at the picnic table. They had a large tent that could probably sleep ten, a canopy tent over the picnic table, and a minivan piled high with pool inflatables. The green and white slices of the beach ball in question were just visible through the back window in the fading daylight.

Tom looked up as we walked closer.

I waved. "How are you this evening? I'm Thea Pagoni, the campground owner," I said. "Tom, right?"

"That's right. And this is my wife and son, Samantha and Hunter." He pointed to them, then stuck out his hand and shook mine with a wide grin. "What can I do you for?"

Hunter walked over and wrapped his arms around Tom's leg.

"You may have heard we had an incident and that the police have been questioning people," I said.

"We did hear, and talked with them earlier," Tom said. "What a horrible thing. I'm just glad the competition went on. My son is a huge cornhole fan, and he would have been so disappointed if they cancelled it."

The boy tugged on Tom's shirt. He leaned down, and Hunter whispered in his ear while pointing at Gar.

"You can pet the puppy if your dad says it's okay," I said. "He's very friendly."

Tom nodded and Hunter hugged Gar, almost disappearing into his thick black hair.

"I'm glad you're enjoying your time here. I see you've been to the pool." I pointed out the huge beach ball in the back of their van.

"Yup."

Hunter resumed his grip on his dad's leg. Tom smiled down at him and ruffled his hair.

"It must've taken a long time to blow that thing up," I said.

"Actually, I saw a great tip in a video of dad hacks for camping. You take a hose and use your car exhaust to blow it up." He crossed his arms and smiled proudly.

"And it worked? Wow." I hoped my fake enthusiasm didn't come off phony.

"It sounds silly, but it did! Blew it up real fast, which was good because someone was a cranky pants and really needed to get in that pool." Tom chuckled and patted Hunter's back.

"Did you get to see all of the competition?" I asked.

"We sure did. We didn't miss a single match, did we, buddy?"

Hunter shook his head hard.

"What about before the competition? Did you get to meet some of the players?"

"We walked around all day talking to them. We even got a corn bag signed."

At the mention of the corn bag, Hunter took off in a hurry and disappeared into the tent.

"Did you see anything suspicious going on?" I asked.

"I racked my brain when I talked to the police, but everyone was just so nice," Tom said.

Hunter returned and proudly held out a yellow corn bag covered in Sharpie signatures.

"Neat," I told him.

Hunter beamed and resumed his hold on his dad's leg with one hand while clutching the corn bag with the other.

"And was Hunter with you the whole time?" I asked.

Samantha, who sat near the fire a few feet away, laughed. "Tom can't even go to the bathroom without Hunter tagging along."

"It's true," Tom admitted with a grin.

I looked at Hennie, who also appeared charmed by the adorable family.

"Daddy's a pretty great guy, huh?" I asked Hunter.

He nodded enthusiastically.

"Well, let me know if you see or hear anything or think of anything that might be interesting," I said.

"Certainly. Anything we can do to help."

Hunter petted Gar one more time before we walked away. When we were far enough, I said to Hennie, "I don't know what Nolan was thinking. There's no way that guy killed Hugo."

"Wouldn't think so."

"Do you think Nolan tried to say Tom was guilty to make himself look less guilty?"

"Didn't though, did it?" Hennie pointed out.

I shook my head. "It makes him seem desperate to clear his name."

We found Tom's neighbors, a young couple named Jen and Seth, sitting at their picnic table, playing cards by a glowing lantern. Like so many other campsites I'd seen in the last few days, they had a cornhole platform in one corner, near their small tent.

When I asked if they'd seen anything, Jen looked over, smiled at Tom, and waved. Then she said, "No, everything has been great."

I wasn't sure, but she seemed to have a slight sarcastic tone that confused me.

Hennie and I turned to walk away, but before I could ask her opinion on Jen, we had to pause as Tom and his family pulled out of their site. Nothing had been packed up, so they must be heading to town for the night. They waved and we waved back, then continued on down Bass Road.

"Thea?"

I turned around to see Jen rushing over to me, her eyebrows pulled together worriedly. Seth was a few feet behind.

She reached us and said, "There's something."

I knew it. "What's going on?"

Jen looked back at Tom's site and hugged her arms around her middle. Seth rubbed her back soothingly.

"That guy is a nut case," Jen said.

"Who, Tom?"

"The guy who just drove off? He went crazy the other day," Jen said.

Seth nodded. "We saw the, umm... victim, Hugo, the day before he died."

Jen launched into the story, waving her hands around for emphasis. "Oh, it was awful. That little boy is over there throwing his corn bag at a platform in their site when Hugo walks by. Tom sees him and gets all excited and points out to his son that it's the head official. Hunter is all excited and rushes over to talk to Hugo, who is not at all interested in talking to him. Tom walks over and says how much his son loves cornhole and how he wants to be a cornhole player when he grows up. And then that—"

"Jerk," Seth filled in.

Jen nodded once. "He actually told Tom—loudly—that his son was a terrible player and would never be a pro. So of course, Hunter bursts into tears. I mean, what is he, four? Horrible. And Tom gets mad—like any dad would— and starts yelling at the guy."

"What did he say?" I asked.

"Just like, 'How dare you talk to my son like that' or something similar," she said. "But then, it didn't end. Hugo tried to walk away, and Tom chased after him, still yelling. I thought they were going to fight."

"They didn't, though?" I clarified.

She shook her head.

"I think Tom would've hit him," Seth added, "but he realized people were around. It was scary, though, the way he snapped. And then, right after, he smiled and acted like nothing had happened and he..." Seth looked to Jen questioningly.

"We felt threatened," she said. "Tom made it seem like if we mentioned the argument, he would do something. That's why we lied at first."

"What did he say to make you feel threatened?" I asked.

Jen shook her head slowly and shivered. "He saw us and grinned this weird, fake smile and said, 'Well now, wasn't he a pleasant man? I'm glad we could talk with him and meet him.' And I just blinked at Tom in shock because he totally lied. He acted like nothing had happened. I guess he thought I might say something. He smiled even more and said to me, 'I'm sure everyone saw how nice of a chat we had with Hugo.' And he kept smiling and staring at me."

Seth jumped in. "It was bizarre, let me tell you. I didn't like the way he looked at Jen, so I just waved and we went inside the tent for a while."

Jen added, "We were so creeped out, I even wanted to change campsites, but the office was too busy."

I gave an apologetic smile. "Sorry about that. It's been a little chaotic with the competition."

Jen nodded. "I understand. And he's been fine since, but I wouldn't want him to know I told you all that. He might flip out on us next."

The couple exchanged a worried glance.

"I'm sorry you had to witness that," I said. "If there's anything I can do to make your stay more enjoyable, let me know. And please, if you see anything else like that, tell me."

"We will," Jen said.

While Tom and his family were out, I talked with the other campers nearby. A few other families confirmed the argument and recalled it almost exactly as Jen had. One dad we talked to also said he overheard Brian say that he wanted Hugo, "Out of the way."

As we headed back toward the office, I told Hennie, "Brian and Ray don't seem any less guilty. And this changes what I thought about Tom."

"I'll say. Never expected that from Tom. Maybe the fight with Hugo continued later," she said.

"The whole thing makes him seem capable of murder."

"Only one problem there," Hennie said. "An angry man will commit an angry crime."

I'd seen enough of that firsthand to know it was true.

"And this wasn't an angry crime," I admitted.

Hennie shook her head. "Highly pre-meditated."

"But Tom was the only one who knew about the car exhaust thing."

"Except for Nolan."

"Right." How could I forget the most obvious suspect?

CHAPTER 6

I left Hennie and returned to the office to check on Sally and Curtis. I'd been out most of the day talking to people and had left them alone. After hearing Jen and Seth complain that the office had been too busy, I felt bad about my absence. It was also nearing time for Sally to go home and for Curtis to head back to his camper for the night.

I entered the office to find a line of campers waiting with not-so-patient expressions. Sally stood behind the counter, talking animatedly. She was apologizing and her eyes looked as frazzled as her hair. Curtis, on the other hand, sat off to the side on his stool, doing a crossword puzzle.

I couldn't believe he would ignore a line like that. "Curtis, is there a reason you're not doing your job?"

He looked up at me slowly and then over to Sally. He gave me a glare, slid off his stool, and shuffled over to the counter to help the next camper.

I stared at him in shock a moment before storming behind the counter to get to my private office. I shut the door and put my head in my hands. What was I going to do about Curtis? What was I going to do about Nolan?

When I had sufficiently calmed down many minutes later, I walked back out. Sally was organizing check-in forms, and Curtis had returned to his puzzle. No campers waited, though a few milled around the store. I inspected Sally. Her face looked red and the hairs near her temple stuck to her head with sweat. Her sleeves were pushed up, and she looked determined as she flipped through folders in the filing cabinet.

"You okay?" I asked.

She nodded once.

"Sorry it's been so crazy. After today, it should slow down. But if you get busy like that, you can ask Curtis for help. And you can always grab the walkie and call me."

"Okay. Thanks." She gave a half smile.

Several squeaky meows came from under the office counter.

"I moved them out here," Sally admitted. "I thought they'd do better if they had someone to play with."

I knelt down to pet the kittens. They tried to walk and tumbled over each other in the soft blanket folds. The evidence of their playfulness was all over Sally's feet and ankles in thin red lines.

"I see their claws are a little sharp," I said.

Sally waved it off. "They like to play rough. Just like my boys."

"Why don't you go on and head home."

"But it's not time yet. I still have a half hour."

"It's okay. It's been a long day."

She picked up her purse but hesitated.

"Sally, I'm not going to tell anyone you left early. Why don't you stop somewhere quiet and take a few minutes for yourself? Your husband won't be expecting you home yet, right?"

"True." She covered her smile with a hand. "I could do that. Some time for myself..." She looked thoughtful.

"Maybe an ice cream cone from Rollie's?" I suggested.

Her face lit up. "They sell alcohol! And chocolate."

"They do."

She clutched her purse close and hurried over to the door, then paused. "Thanks Thea! Mommy's gonna have a good night."

"Just be safe!"

The bell over the door jingled, and she was gone.

I returned to my office to think. Normally, I saw Nolan multiple times throughout the day, so I always had an idea of what had gotten done and what was going on. But between the cornhole competition and me avoiding him, I hadn't seen him much.

I grabbed the walkie to call him. "Hey, where are you?"

"At the lake. What do you need?"

"The lake? Are you off duty?"

He huffed. "Hardly. I'm cleaning up puke. In the sand."

"Oh. Do you need anything?"

"Nope."

"Everything looking okay?"

"Yup."

"I'm closing the office a few minutes early. I'll be at Hennie's if you need me."

"You figure out that I'm not a murderer yet?" he asked.

"Uhh, still working on that."

I said nothing more, and neither did he.

As Gar and I walked toward Hennie's, I had a thought. And this would be the safest time to do it if Nolan was busy at the lake, across the campground.

I stopped, whistled to Gar who had gone to chase a toad, and turned the opposite way. When we got to Nolan's campsite, I took my time searching around.

His camper door was locked and I didn't want to break in. His porch contained a few tools caked in mud, a pair of old boots, and a hatchet.

I was ready to turn back and give up when something glinted in the light. I bent to look closer and saw a thumbtack. Its end was a dark green ball. I'd chosen those tacks because they matched the Cedar Fish logo colors. The rest of the tacks held flyers and notices on the office corkboard.

I took photos and decided it was time to get out of there. Gar followed me as I tried to reason out why Nolan would have that tack. I'd noticed one was missing days ago. Had it been the day of the competition or the day before? I couldn't recall.

I opened the photo of the crime scene and zoomed in on the holes in the air mattress. No, they were bigger than a tack, weren't they? Only problem with that reasoning was that when I'd first seen the holes, my initial thought was that they had been made with a thumbtack.

I felt slightly dizzy as we headed back toward Hennie's. I couldn't shake the thought that I'd just found possible evidence and that even the police suspected Nolan was the killer.

I walked slowly, Gar trotting along at my side as always. I had put his Cedar Fish Campground t-shirt on him for the competition and he still wore it, though it was now covered in grass stains and dirt smears. "You had fun today, didn't you?" At least someone had. I petted his head and he licked me in agreement.

Hennie saw us approaching and called out, "Just in time!"

"For?"

"Beer and karate."

Gar saw Hennie's black cat, Midnight, sitting on the porch and took off after her. Then Zack, the Husky, perked up from his nap and joined in the chase.

"They'll be fine." Hennie waved them off and I followed her inside.

She handed me a beer, then promptly punched me in the stomach with a light tap. I jerked back and spilled beer on the floor.

"Gotta be ready for anything," she said.

"I guess I didn't expect my friend to attack me." I got a paper towel from the kitchen to wipe up my mess.

"Let's do more attack moves," Hennie said.

We spent most of an hour taking turns trying to punch or grab each other and breaking free. I had learned a lot from her, but I still felt far from able to protect myself well. And the fear that I couldn't stop an attack only heightened the fear I felt about Nolan. If I was wrong about him and he turned violent on me, it would be far worse than anything Russell was capable of.

"The more I think about it," I said as I kicked the punching bag, "the more it pisses me off. Tom lied to us." Another kick. "He didn't mention a thing about his argument. And he told the witnesses not to mention it? That makes him look very guilty."

Hennie stepped in and punched the bag twice, then kicked it. "Exactly. Maybe Nolan was right about him after all."

"Tom didn't come back yet, so I couldn't ask him about it. And I don't know that Ray or Brian didn't do it, either. And there's always Nolan." I punched the bag several

times, the anger and anxiety pouring from me as I hit it
with all my strength.

"That's right, honey. You get it all out. Don't forget to
twist into it."

"I can't believe this is happening again! I don't want to
solve another murder! I don't want more man troubles!" I
yelled as I beat the bag relentlessly with my fists.

"Go on," Hennie said. She got behind the bag stand and
held it. "Now kick."

I kicked the bag over and over until the fury faded with
my energy. I kicked one final time with a loud "hi-yah" and
then stepped back, breathing hard. I sat down on the hard-
wood of her cabin floor.

"Why does my life keep falling apart?" I wiped my
sweaty forehead on my sleeve. "It's like no matter what I
do, I keep facing the same issues again and again."

"That's how it is. Life is just a series of patterns." Hennie handed me a fresh beer and plopped down beside me.
"What you gotta do is break the pattern."

"Right. I can't let what happened with my ex ever happen again."

Hennie looked confused. "I thought you were upset
over there being another murder."

"I am. But I'm more upset that Nolan isn't turning out
to be who I thought he was."

"That happened before?"

I nodded. "Russell was the most charming man you
ever met. Until you crossed him. The first time he got mad

at me, I couldn't believe it. I thought he just had a bad night. But it kept getting worse after that. And then when he got violent..." I sucked in a breath and the rage flared again. "I guess that's when I finally had enough. I can't have that happen again. I can't find out that Nolan is really this aggressive person who I thought was kind."

"I hate to say it, but being a vet and a former cop, I'm sure he's been plenty aggressive. That doesn't make him unkind, though. And it doesn't mean he'd turn that on you. Aggression has its place."

I gave her a harsh sideway look. "Any man who can commit violence against another person is capable of doing it again."

"You have to take into account the reason a man turns violent in the first place. Sometimes life calls for that, and if you don't stand up to it, you get knocked down."

"He was fired from the police force. There was an investigation and everything. And I'm wondering if it wasn't because he went out of control on the job one day."

"Have you asked him?"

I shook my head.

"Still avoiding him?"

"Maybe." I sighed. "I don't even know if he should be working at Cedar Fish. What happens if it gets out that our security guard is a murder suspect? I don't think people will feel safe." I couldn't bring myself to tell her about the thumbtack. I hadn't decided if it was really evidence or not.

"I wouldn't go acting on suspicion. You do need a security guard more than ever."

"What I need are employees who actually work. I found Curtis doing a crossword puzzle today while Sally was frantic and there were three people in line. I don't know what to do with him anymore. It doesn't seem right to fire him, but I can't pay someone to do puzzles all day when we need the help so badly."

"You're not in the wrong to fire someone for not doing their job."

"But he was friends with my grandparents. They hired him, and he's worked there for his whole retirement."

"Maybe there's something better he could do than work in the office."

"Like what?"

She thought for a moment. "Well, I'm not sure. But you keep thinking on it and something will come to mind."

After I collected Gar, we walked back to the office. I sat in the near dark, hanging my hand over the box of kittens to play with them. Gar watched eagerly, but obeyed when I told him to sit and not go after them.

The black and white kitten grabbed my finger and bit it. I yanked my hand back in shock. I petted the grey and white one and received a long scratch along my pinkie as a reward.

"Why is everyone so violent?" I stood up, disgusted. "Come on, Gar. We need some rest and relaxation."

CHAPTER 7

Since I hadn't seen Tom again to ask about the argument with Hugo, I decided to visit his campsite first thing in the morning. After drinking a cup of coffee and forcing myself to wait until a decent hour, I filled my mug with ice cubes and headed out.

Gar bounded ahead of me, jumping up to swat at a moth, then chasing after a chipmunk as it skittered across the dirt road. When we neared Tom's site, Hunter ran toward Gar, squealing in excitement. Hunter threw a stick for him, which gave me the perfect in to talk to Tom.

"Hi again."

I waved at Tom and Samantha, who sat drinking coffee from metal mugs by their campfire. They smiled as they watched Hunter and Gar playing.

"You have any pets at home?" I asked.

"No, but we're considering getting a dog after seeing this," Samantha said.

"Sure would make him happy," Tom added.

"It'd be good protection, too," I said. "If anyone ever gave you trouble, your dog would be there to defend you." Tom nodded and I abandoned any subtly. "Like, if a cornhole official insults your son and you get into an argument with him."

I watched Tom's face. At first, his smile stayed in place, but then it became clear that he was forcing it.

"Is there a reason you didn't mention your fight with Hugo?"

He looked straight ahead and kept smiling. "Just didn't seem important. We talked and settled things like adults."

"And you didn't think having an altercation with a murder victim hours before his death might be relevant?"

"Hugo started it," Samantha said sharply.

Tom patted her knee and let out a stifled chuckle. "Was it those silly neighbors across the road?" He looked over, his grin seeming more menacing by the second. "And after they promised not to bring it up." He shook his head. "You can't blame me for defending my son."

"No, and Hugo was quite a rude person," I said. "I'm sure it wasn't entirely uncalled for."

"Exactly," Samantha said.

Tom seemed to relax. "There, you see. It's perfectly *normal*. So normal, I didn't even think to mention it." He chuckled again.

Hunter ran back over to Tom and nuzzled his head into his lap before returning to Gar.

Tom looked at me. "I would never get violent in front of Hunter. That would set a horrible example."

"It wasn't a particularly violent murder."

Samantha sucked in a breath and gave Tom a concerned look. He patted her knee again. "Honey, I would never *kill* someone." He turned back to me. "You admitted yourself he was rude. He could have angered any number of people."

"Anyone you can think of in particular?"

They both looked thoughtful. Probably trying their hardest to pin the guilt somewhere else.

"Not that I can think of," Tom said.

"You didn't overhear anyone saying they disliked Hugo or wanted him dead?"

"Lots of people seemed to dislike him," Tom admitted, "but I didn't hear anyone talk about killing him. Though, there is one thing that might be strange."

"What's that?" I asked.

"That security guard? The one who drives the black truck around all the time? He saw me with the beach ball and flipped out, saying how dangerous it was. I hadn't thought much of it, but he warned that if I had the ball in an enclosed space and it leaked, it could harm someone. I never thought of it until he said that." Tom shrugged. "I don't know what that means, but it's all I can think of."

My stomach churned. "Thanks for letting me know. You all have a good day."

I called for Gar and chomped a piece of ice as I continued on my way. Nolan again. And I might have just put Jen and Seth in danger.

I'd talked to Hennie the night before, but I needed someone to talk to again. I wasn't used to not being able to call Nolan to discuss things about the campground or the murder. Last time tragedy struck at Cedar Fish, he'd been right there with me, helping me figure things out. Now, I felt very much alone, trying to figure out who Nolan Cade really was.

I thought about going to see Hennie again, but on Sunday mornings, she went to church. I went with her once or twice before, but had too much on my mind that day to get anything out of it. Nolan was likely making rounds. He usually took his days off—not that he was really ever off— in the middle of the week, since weekends were our busier time. Most days, he started with patrols and whatever needed tending to from the day or night before.

Sally would be in by now, and I thought it might be nice to sit and chat with her a while. I hadn't gotten to know her well. Maybe she loved to read mystery novels in her spare time and had a good sleuthing mind.

The office door was unlocked, but no one stood behind the counter. "Sally?"

"Down here!"

I walked around the counter and found her on the floor, the three kittens cuddled in her arms. She rocked back and forth, cradling them and singing lullabies. I waited until she finished "Rock a Bye Baby," but when she next broke into "You Are my Sunshine," I decided to leave her to her private concert.

I checked the reservations and saw that Jen and Seth were checking out that day. They should be safe, then. I left a note for Nolan at the front counter to keep an eye on their campsite until they had gone.

A few supplies were running low, and I hadn't seen Enid in a while. She went to the early, early church service and opened the store after. By now, she'd be there.

I walked out of the office and Nolan walked toward me. Unease bubbled in my chest and I hurried away, pretending I hadn't seen him. I hopped in my car, called for Gar to join me, and we took off. Just seeing the glowing sign for Rollie's a mile later made me feel better.

When I stepped over Sunny Boy to enter the store, Gar stopped to sniff him. Enid saw us come in and called out, "Hi there, Thea! Just made a fresh pot of coffee." She got up and vanished into the backroom for a moment before returning with a fresh steaming mug.

I wrapped my hands around it. "You always know what I need."

Enid smiled. "What's on your mind, dear?"

"Ugg." I leaned my elbows on the counter and told her everything that I'd been worrying over lately. Another murder, more lost business for the campground, Nolan possibly being the murderer, everything feeling like it was falling apart, and even my Curtis woes.

Enid listened attentively. "It's hard to think someone might not be who you thought or who you want them to be."

"It feels all too familiar," I added.

"Maybe life is telling you something. Maybe you need to stop trying to make everything how you want it and enjoy how it is."

There were my old control issues, coming back again. After so many hours of therapy learning how to let things go, I'd only exchanged one set of problems for another.

"I need to know if Nolan is a murderer before I can enjoy anything. I'm afraid to be around him right now."

"That's understandable. Have the police said anything?"

"They said he was a suspect, but we haven't gotten any updates." The thumbtack poked at my mind, and I swatted it away.

Enid tsked. "You'd think after you caught their killer last time, they'd give you a little more courtesy."

"You'd think. Maybe they're mad I showed them up."

"Then I guess you'll have to do it again."

"I've tried," I said. "I've talked to everyone I could, and no one knows much. Everyone hated Hugo. Lots of people had motive and opportunity to kill him."

"I can see why everyone hated him. He came in here and was a real twerp. I almost kicked him out."

I put my chin in my hand. "What am I going to do?"

"I don't know about this murder, but I can help your Curtis situation. Maybe."

"Yeah?" I looked up at her hopefully.

"I had a problem like that one time. Had this woman who worked the post office counter, but she would get short and snippy with people, even though she did a fine job. Was a good worker and everything, but caused some problems. So, when me and Rollie put our heads together, we thought, you know, her attitude would do just fine in the bar where the crowd gets a little rough at times. We suggested it to her and though she wasn't thrilled at the time, she loved bartending and was happy to show some cleavage if it meant more tips."

"Hennie suggested something like that—giving him a different role—but I'm not sure what else Curtis could do. He can barely move and he can't lift or stand long."

Enid squinted thoughtfully. "You said he's always doing puzzles. That means his mind is sharp, even if his body isn't. How are his eyes?"

"Okay, I think. He wears reading glasses, but that's it."

"So, he can see, hear, and think, even if he can't move well or lift. A lifeguard would be perfect, so long as no one needed to be saved."

The answer clicked into my mind. "Oh! He could patrol! Granted, as a security guard, he'd need to at least carry a weapon, and he'd have to call Nolan if anything came up since he couldn't physically do much, but he could ride the golf cart and look out for suspicious activity. I don't think his hearing is too bad."

Enid clapped her hands. "There you go! See."

I smiled, feeling some relief for the first time in days. "Thanks, Enid. Having you here is almost like having Grandma back."

"Almost." Enid winked, and I gave her a quick hug.

There was a lightness in my step, despite my fresh wave of grief, as I got back into my car. This would solve two problems. It would make Curtis more productive, but it would also mean another set of eyes watching the campground. If Nolan was up to something, Curtis might catch it. And if Nolan was guilty, I'd need someone to do security.

When we got back to the campground, I parked at my cabin and called Gar to hop out. The backseat was covered in muddy paw prints. Gar didn't chew the seatbelts or anything like that, but my car was getting slowly destroyed by driving around the campground with all of its rocks and dirt. If I would be transporting a puppy regularly and lived in a campground, it was time to get a more appropriate vehicle. The Lexus had to go.

I'd considered selling it before, when I first realized how tight our cash-flow was. The car would bring in a decent chunk of change. If it kept getting ruined, though, I'd lose money. With my mind made up to place an ad, Gar and I went to the old equipment shed.

The key barely turned in the rusty lock of the shed. I yanked the door hard to get it open and was greeted with a whiff of musty air. I felt around for the switch, getting at least two splinters before turning on the light.

Several gas cans sat to one side, hedge clippers and trimmers hung on the wall, and in the back, behind the mower and weed whacker, sat the old golf cart. It needed some work, and I hadn't been concerned about it since Nolan was fine with patrolling in his truck. I pushed the cart out into the sunlight and tried to start it. The key did nothing in the ignition.

I called to Nolan on the walkie. "Hey, I got the old golf cart out. I need you to take a look at it and get it running."

"What for?"

"We're going to use it."

"I'll get to it tomorrow. I'm mucking out the pond today."

"Actually, the pond can wait. This is a priority."

He paused. "Why? Did your car break down?"

"It's not for me. Curtis will be doing security."

Nolan laughed. "Right. Put Sally in charge of running the place, and we can take off into the sunset."

"I'm serious. Curtis is going to ride on the cart to do patrols."

"What?" he snapped.

"I can't pay him to sit and do puzzles all day."

"So you decided that since he can't physically do much, he should have one of the most physically demanding jobs in the campground?"

"No. If there's a problem, he'll call you to handle it. He'd just be patrolling."

"Checking up on me, you mean."

"No," I said too fast and too sharp.

He harrumphed. "Nice, Thea. Real nice."

CHAPTER 8

I stared across my kitchen table at the flaky, chocolate creation I'd made. After my success with the keftedakia, I decided to try another of Enid's favorite recipes. A dessert this time—chocolate baklava. It had now been two nights since I made it and it still sat, untouched, in the glass 9 x 13 pan.

I guess it had turned out okay. Everything went well during the baking process, and I had no reason to think it would taste bad. The problem was, when I'd gotten the recipe, I planned to share the dessert with Nolan. I couldn't justify baking an entire baklava to eat alone. Sally stayed away from sweets—or at least tried—and Curtis wasn't allowed to have them for health reasons. I could coax Hennie into a piece or two, but she'd made a comment once about Enid's food always being "weird," so I wasn't sure she'd even try it.

But Nolan would love it as much as I expected to. He'd eat half the pan and want more. And he'd probably want vanilla ice cream to go with it. Which was why I had an unopened tub in my freezer. I wanted to call him. I'd made the dessert to share, and I wanted to share it with him. I wanted to talk to him. I wanted to hear him strum a song on his guitar or watch him play with Gar.

Yet, every time I reached for my walkie or phone, I stopped. I couldn't be sure of him, and until I was, I couldn't be alone with him. And there was no way I was going to dig into such a huge and delicious-smelling dessert when I felt lonely and stressed. So, my hard work sat there, waiting. Sad little dessert that no one dared to eat.

Gar watched from his bed with pain in his eyes. His tail flopped back and forth and he licked his chops again and again.

I put the cover back on my pan and returned it to the fridge. Hopefully, it would keep until I figured out if Nolan was a murderer or not.

"Alright." I put my hands on my knees and stood in front of Gar. "What do you say to a walk?"

At the word "walk," his ears twitched, and he got to his feet. He barked in anticipation.

"Let's go!"

Gar dashed to the door, barely halting before sliding into it. He waited for me to catch up, his pink tongue lolling from his mouth.

We stepped out into the crisp evening air. Around me, crickets and frogs made percussive songs of their clicks and chirps. A bullfrog, likely from the pond, added a sporadic bass note. Gar's feet crunched along the gravel with my own, swishes of tiny stones filling in the remaining space in the evening song.

I didn't keep Gar on a leash, though I had posted a leash notice for dogs out of their campsites. He was still a puppy, but his training had gone well, and he was already quite obedient and smart. He was great with children, of course, and had plenty of other animals to investigate and play with. Most people and creatures alike found it difficult not to become enamored by his friendliness, thick black hair, and teddy bear-like face.

As we continued on our stroll, taking in the world around us, I heard shouting in the distance. Gar growled and I picked up my pace.

I called to Nolan on the walkie. "Where are you?"

When he didn't respond, I broke into a jog. Gar easily matched my pace.

The shouting grew louder. It had to be several men, possibly getting into a fight. When the campers in question came into view, I saw that three men stood in a tight circle, shuffling back and forth as they tried to pull each other apart.

"Hey!" I shouted.

Gar barked loudly several times.

I reached the brawl as Nolan pushed Brian back, away from the third man.

At first, I thought Nolan had stepped in to break things up. Doing his job. But then I caught sight of the shiner at his right eye.

Nolan stood between the men, who continued to lunge forward, shouting at each other. Brian's mouth bled and his lip had swollen. The third guy had a torn shirt and bruises around his eyes. He held his stomach and looked to be in pain.

"I'm calling the police," I said.

Nolan said to Brian, "Now just take a step back and cool down."

"Outer Branson Police Department," the woman on the phone said.

"I need someone to come to Cedar Fish Campground. We've had a physical assault."

I gave the dispatcher the details, and she promised to send someone right away. Which would be at least twenty minutes.

Brian stood off to one side of the campsite and the other man stood across from him. Nolan and I now stood between them, at least ten feet separating us from each man.

"Were you part of this?" I asked Nolan.

"I broke things up," he said.

"That lunatic attacked me!" Brian pointed to the other man.

Nolan jerked his head toward the man in question and said, "That's Juan Vega, the second-place winner."

"It wasn't my fault!" Juan said. "He hit me first."

"What did you see?" I asked Nolan.

"They were yelling at each other when I walked up. I don't know who started it."

"You started it by getting involved." Brian glared at Nolan. "If you hadn't laid a hand on me, I wouldn't have hit you."

I raised an eyebrow at Nolan. He shook his head. Was he seriously involved in this thing? My chest tightened to think he'd gotten into something violent when I was trying so hard to believe he wasn't.

"The police can decide who's at fault," Nolan said.

"It's a good thing we have back-up security," I said quietly enough that only Nolan would hear. "Since you'll be off getting questioned by the police. Again."

"Yeah, Curtis would have been a real help. I was the one who *broke up* the fight," Nolan said.

"Not according to Brian."

Nolan gave me an incredulous glower. "And you believe him over me? You think I started the fight by trying to calm things down?"

I shrugged. And then I blurted, "I mean, I did find a thumbtack at your campsite." My hands shook waiting for his response.

"A thumbtack?" He glared and put a hand on his hip. "And that means what, exactly?"

I almost couldn't get the words out through my dry throat, but I needed to keep my voice low enough that Brian and Juan wouldn't hear all the details of our conversation. "It's the size of the holes in the air mattress. Maybe it means you were the one who put them there." I studied his reaction closely.

"Are you serious right now?"

"Then tell me why it was there. What possible reason could a tack have for being on your porch?"

He gritted his teeth and said, "Maybe because I found it stuck in the tread of my work boot and yanked it out, then tossed it there, not thinking you'd go searching my place, find it, and use it to accuse me of murder."

Okay, well, that explanation did make sense. The tack might've fallen out of the corkboard. Nolan was around the office most days, so he could have stepped on it, and the treads on his boots were thick enough that it wouldn't have gone through to his foot.

It was a small relief to have an answer, but he could be lying. And even if his story was true, it didn't mean he hadn't also used the tack for the holes. "Okay, well, I guess the police will determine that, like you said."

"Unbelievable, Thea." He balled his hands into fists. "I'm going up front to wait for the cops. Keep your campers under control."

Nolan walked off. Curtis had gone back to his camper for the night hours ago. I considered calling Hennie, who would have gladly come with a gun or two to make sure nothing else happened, but Brian and Juan seemed to be somewhat settled down. At least they stayed several feet apart and didn't try to go for each other. I wished I'd brought my pepper spray along, but I had Gar at my side, and he was good protection or intervention.

When the police finally arrived, I talked to Officer Randall while Longshore talked with Brian.

"What happened here?" Randall asked.

"I didn't see anything except Nolan trying to keep them apart," I told him.

Randall nodded and made a note. "Do you want either of them removed from the property?" He waved his notepad toward Brian and Juan.

As much as I wanted to avoid another altercation, I might need them close for questioning. "I don't think that's necessary as long as they're calmed down."

Randall nodded and made another note. "Have you had any other problems with those two?"

"No."

"I think that's all I need from you," he said.

"How's the... other case going?"

He tilted his head side to side. "Going."

"Do you have any solid leads?"

"A few suspects we're looking into."

"Is Nolan still one of them?" *Please say no. Please say no.*

"I can't say." He looked back over his shoulder. "Just be careful, Thea. This campground doesn't seem to be the safest place."

I pressed my lips together. No use trying to argue when I didn't disagree. "Did Nolan have anything to do with this fight? Was he involved?"

"You told us he was involved."

"I mean, did he participate?"

"He's not getting arrested."

"Good."

I headed back to the office to wait for them to finish. Some time later, when I saw the cruiser turn out of the campground, I walked outside. Nolan stood on the office porch, watching them go.

"Glad you didn't get arrested," I said.

He turned with a glare. "Why would I? They arrested Juan for assaulting Brian."

"Why'd he do it?"

"Said Brian cheated. I went to Ray's cabin and talked to him about it."

I nodded.

"Juan reported his allegation," Nolan continued. "The world officials are coming to investigate. They have to have the rightful winner before the big championship, according to Ray."

I nodded again. "I had no idea cornhole was so serious."

"None of the ranking players or those involved can leave until the officials have made the call," Nolan said. "So

I'll keep a close eye on Brian and Juan, when he gets back. Unless you want Curtis to do it."

"No, I would appreciate you watching them. Thanks," I said.

"When I talked to Ray, I also took a photo of his tires. Did you bother to compare the treads to the photos from the scene?"

I recalled taking the photos at Ray's cabin, but with everything that had been going on, I'd forgotten to check. I didn't want to admit my slip, but I couldn't lie, either.

"I guess you're not too motivated to clear my name," he said. "Because the fact that Ray's tires match the tracks at the murder scene might say something."

"They do?" My eyes widened.

Nolan nodded once. "I did more of your sleuthing for you on Tom Adkins, too. I got a background report on the guy. Lots of violence in his past. I'll forward you the email."

I blinked in surprise. After talking to Tom's neighbors, I knew he had a temper, but I didn't expect him to have a record. "What sort of violence?"

"Street fights mostly. And domestic violence."

A spike of cold fear shot through me. "Did he hurt Samantha?"

Nolan shook his head. "At least not on paper. He had some trouble with a few past girlfriends, though."

"The couple at the site across from Tom said he snapped and argued with Hugo."

"I know."

"Oh."

His eyes narrowed. "Hennie still talks to me."

My head hung with guilt, and I thought of my lonely baklava. "I've just been... busy."

"You're as bad a liar as Tom," he said.

Tom was lying? Had I missed something when I talked to him?

"Thea." He stood directly in front of me and wore his most serious face. "Tom has a violent past. He was seen using car exhaust to blow up a beach ball, which was the same method used to kill Hugo. The fight with Hugo over his son gives him motive, especially for a guy known to snap. He had opportunity, too."

"But there's nothing tying him to the scene. And it wasn't a particularly violent murder."

"It takes a violent heart to kill someone. And there isn't much at the scene tying anyone."

"Except you."

He stared at me for a long moment, his eyes searching mine. I had to step back and look away.

"Tom does look guilty," I admitted. "He didn't tell me he has a violent past. But if that's true, then we have to find whatever evidence there is. Get a better idea of his timeline. Do the police know what time the mattress was tampered with?"

"They speculate late afternoon."

"How do you know that?"

He raised an eyebrow. "I have a few connections."

"I didn't think you wanted help from your brothers or father."

"It's a bit different when I'm one of the suspects. They're doing all they can to get me cleared."

"So am I," I said defensively.

He huffed. "Yeah, you and your thumbtack are doing a fine job. Good thing you went into corporate law. If you'd been a criminal lawyer, innocent people might be in jail."

I shot a glare back at him. "I'm doing everything I can."

I stormed off and had to call to Gar to make him follow me. "We have to figure this out fast," I said to Gar as I headed home.

There was one thing I could do right at that moment. It had gotten darker, but was still evening. I tapped my pocket and felt my pepper spray. Time to start carrying it on me. I planned to get a can for my office as well. I'd also been practicing some Tang Soo Do moves Hennie taught me. She might be right about me needing my own punching bag. Maybe I could put one in the corner of my living room.

I neared Tom's campsite and heard footsteps behind me. I assumed it was campers. In mid-June, the place was busy, and people walked along the gravel roads and paths at all hours. But these footsteps were fast and heavy.

I turned as Nolan caught up to me. "What are you doing?" he hissed. "You're going to talk to a potential killer alone?"

"Aren't I alone with a potential killer right now?" I forced a chuckle, but it fell flat.

"You're not being careful."

"I'm armed."

He slid his hand across my back and around my waist. I thought he was hugging me, but he pulled his arm back without any sort of squeeze.

"No, you're not. Pepper spray doesn't count."

"I also have my self-defense moves."

"Right."

We reached the campsite where Tom and his family sat around a fire, roasting marshmallows. Samantha and Hunter held one stick while Tom held another.

"It's fine," I said to Nolan under my breath. "Please go."

"Hi again," Tom said, waving to us.

"Hi there. I wondered if I might talk to you for a minute?" I asked.

Tom set his stick down and walked toward Nolan and I. "Everything okay?"

I nodded. "I just wondered why you didn't mention to me that you had a violent past."

Tom took a step back and raised his eyebrows in surprise. Nolan shifted one foot back and held himself straighter.

Tom shook his head. "No one wants to be judged by their past. That was another time and another me. I guess I didn't bring it up because I'm so different now that it feels like that was someone else. When I became a dad, everything changed. I'm fully reformed. No more violence." His mouth stretched into a wide grin.

As if to prove his point, Hunter ran to him and grabbed onto his leg. "The marshmallow's done. Can we make s'mores now, Daddy?"

"Sure, buddy. As soon as I'm done talking."

"When was the last time you got into a fight?" I asked.

"It's been about four years."

Hunter dashed to the picnic table and retrieved a package of chocolate bars and graham crackers. He eagerly thrust them at his dad, who took them and thanked the boy. Tom smiled at him and promised, "Soon."

My anger at Tom's omission faded as I watched him with his son. He seemed like a genuinely nice guy.

He juggled the chocolate and graham crackers until Samantha walked over to take them from him.

"Everything okay?" she asked.

"Oh sure," Tom said. "They're just making sure we're okay."

When she walked away, I leaned in and asked, "Your wife does know about your record, right?"

"Of course. And she knows the new me and trusts me."

"Even though the new you still yells at people like Hugo?"

"I'm going to defend my family." Tom shrugged. "I could've hit the guy, but I didn't. Old me would have."

"Daddy!" Hunter held up a sticky glob of a s'more and happily took a bite.

Hunter was the best proof of Tom's claim. If Tom was violent toward or around him, it would show in the way Hunter interacted with him.

"You better get over there," I said with a chuckle.

"Have a good night," Tom said and returned to his fire.

Nolan followed when Gar and I walked away.

"There is no way that guy did it," I said. "His kid won't let him be more than a few feet away. How would he have had enough time to get into Hugo's tent, deflate the air mattress, re-inflate it with car exhaust, then poke holes in it and get back without anyone noticing? That would take at least a half hour."

"Hunter is about four?" Nolan asked.

I nodded.

"Don't four-year-olds still take naps?"

"You seriously think that Ned Flanders back there killed Hugo? Based on the fact that he watched some dad-hack video and yelled at someone known for being a total jerk?"

"Don't forget his violent past."

"A past that is gone now."

"You really think people can change? If that innocent 'Ned Flanders' as you called him had the rap sheet of evil Mr. Burns, would you still think he's so innocent?"

I narrowed my eyes at Nolan. "What about the violence in your past? Does it make you guilty, too? Does that mean you haven't changed?"

His stare turned cold. "That's different."

I forced a laugh. "Of course it is." I turned sharply to walk away from him. "If you think he's such a threat, make sure you keep an eye on him, too."

CHAPTER 9

I wanted to go to bed, but didn't think I had a chance of sleeping. Instead, I headed toward the office, intending to review video footage and my notes. If it hadn't been so late, I would have gone to talk to Ray about his tire tracks. Had I really been so distracted that I hadn't even thought to see if they matched the tracks at the scene?

When Gar and I stepped inside the office, his head snapped to attention. He sniffed the air and moved closer to the office counter, eventually sniffing his way behind.

I stayed back to watch and wait, but when he barked and whined, I went to see what was going on. Dill and her kittens lay in the blanket-lined box under the counter. I bent down to pet them. Dill picked her head up weakly and let out a pained meow.

"What's wrong, Dilly?" I scratched under her chin, but instead of pushing her head forward as she usually did, it fell back to the blanket.

The more I looked at her, the faster my heart pounded. Her fur had a dull appearance, and she looked too skinny. She started to pant. I checked her food and water, and both were full. Did that mean she hadn't eaten or drank, or did it mean Sally filled them recently?

I set the bowl of water in the box, right next to Dill's head. She reached for it with obvious strain, but was unable to take a drink.

I took out my phone and called the person who could help me most. "Hennie, I need you. Something is wrong with Dill."

The call was short and so was the time it took her to get to us. Hennie rushed into the office and joined me on the floor. She petted Dill and looked her over, moving limbs and pressing her hand to Dill's belly. She gently pulled the skin behind Dill's neck and it sank slowly into place.

Hennie shook her head. "How long has she been acting funny?"

"I—Is she sick?"

"Dehydrated."

"I tried to get her to drink, but she couldn't."

Hennie put her hand under Dill's head. "Poor old girl. So, how long?"

"Uhh... I don't really know." My stomach tightened as I thought back. "I guess I've been so busy with the murder and competition that I... I didn't notice."

My throat thickened and Hennie put her arm over my shoulders.

"She's a real old cat, honey, and having kittens ain't easy. But I think we can get her feeling better."

"What do we do?"

"Let's get her to someplace more comfortable." Hennie groaned as she stood.

I carried the box containing Dill and her kittens while Hennie carried the food and water and Gar walked between us. Inside my cabin, we moved the coffee table and created a nest of blankets and pillows in the middle of the living room floor. Gar lay at one side of the pile, as if taking his place as their guard.

"I know you have ice," Hennie said. "Why don'tcha put some cubes in a bowl for her? She can lick easier than she can drink."

I did as Hennie said and then sat between her and Gar. Dill licked at the cubes a little before lying back down.

"We'll just need to keep on her," Hennie said. "Do you still have that bottle from when Ricky was a baby?"

The kitchen cabinet that held my miscellaneous cups and plastic containers had fallen into disarray. It took a minute of searching, but I came across the bottle in the back of the cabinet. I rinsed it and filled it with cool water.

Hennie coaxed Dill into opening her mouth, but she wasn't too eager to drink from the rubber tip. After trying for a while, Hennie set the bottle down with a sigh.

"There's a decent vet in Branson you can take her to in the morning," Hennie said.

I nodded. "I'll call first thing. What about an all-night emergency vet?"

"Isn't one that I know of. Unless you want to drive for hours to the big city. She drank some, so that's a good sign. We just need to keep it going."

For several hours, we took turns trying to get Dill to drink from the bottle or her bowl or to lick the ice cubes. I crushed some ice at one point, wondering if that would help. Dill ate a few small pieces and was spent.

The hour grew late, but Hennie showed no signs of giving up. I dozed on the couch and woke a few hours later to find Hennie asleep on the floor. I spent several minutes getting Dill to drink more before drifting back off.

I hadn't gotten more than a few hours' sleep, but when the morning light streamed in through the windows, I couldn't keep my eyes shut any longer.

I yawned and slid down to the floor.

"Morning, girl." My watch said 7:36. It would likely be another hour and a half until the vet was in.

Gar lay in a half moon, cradling Dill's body at his center. The three kittens snuggled into their mama's soft middle.

I stroked Dill's head to wake her. "Time to drink, Dilly." She didn't move. I picked up the bottle and nudged it at her mouth. Nothing. I put my hand on her stomach, and the stillness woke some deep chill inside me.

"No, no, no!"

"What?" Hennie sat up suddenly and looked around in confusion. Then she saw me and rubbed her face. "How is she?"

My lip quivered and tears rose in my eyes.

Hennie put her hand under Dill's head and felt its heaviness. "Old girl." She shook her head. "I'm so sorry."

"It's all my fault!" The tears came as a flood, mixing with my exhaustion, and I covered my face. "I should have paid closer attention. I should have known something was wrong with her."

Hennie rubbed my back. "She's old, honey. I don't even know how she had kittens, but it took everything she had left. Don't beat yourself up. It's been busy. They look peaceful, don't they?"

They had, but my crying alerted Gar, who now watched me with concern. He eased himself away from the cats. The kittens woke and meowed. Gar came to my side and sat against my legs.

"My grandmother loved that cat," I said. "Dill always slept in the office, and the campers loved her, too."

"Now they can be together," Hennie said.

I sucked in a slow, trembling breath. "I need to call Nolan."

I lifted the walkie talkie off the charger and pressed the button. "You up and about?"

"For hours now," he said sharply.

I ignored his tone. "Can you bring a shovel to my cabin?"

"Why? Need to bury another dead body?" His sarcasm only helped to solidify the numbness in my chest.

"Yes," I said flatly.

His lack of response told me he was already on his way, hurrying to find out what was going on. A few minutes later, I heard his truck door shut. He must've been worried if he drove over.

When he knocked, I called out, "Come in!"

"What's going on?" He stood with shovel in hand at the edge of the living room, looking at us.

"Dill didn't make it," I said.

Her kittens had realized something was not right and grew more frantic in their meowing.

Nolan's shoulders slumped. "I'm sorry."

I shooed the kittens away and cradled Dill in my arms. "Can you bury her by the big oak? That was my grandma's favorite tree."

"Sure." He nodded and his expression was sympathetic.

While Nolan dug the hole, I wrapped Dill in an old blanket. It was stained, worn, and torn, but it was my grandmother's, and she had loved the now-faded floral design. Hennie and I walked outside, and we watched Nolan while I held Dill's body. When Nolan finished digging, he nodded to me.

"Dill, you were a great cat and a great friend." I hugged her body one last time before setting her down in the ground. I picked a handful of dill from my grandmother's herb garden nearby and sprinkled it on top of Dill's body. She'd been named for her love of the plant and could often be found in the garden.

I watched in a numb daze as Hennie tied two thick sticks together with a piece of twine to form a cross. When Nolan had filled the hole, she stuck the cross in to mark the spot. They stood beside me, and I knew they expected me to do or say something.

Nolan awkwardly patted my shoulder. "Anything else I can do?"

"No," I said in a whisper.

Hennie hugged me and we stood there for several silent minutes.

"I need to catch some shuteye." Hennie yawned and rubbed my shoulders. "I'll check in with y'all later."

She walked off, and the tears filled my eyes again.

"Were you up all night?" Nolan asked.

I nodded. "We had to keep making Dill drink."

He was quiet for a long moment. "It's hard losing a pet. Do you want to...?"

When he didn't continue, I looked over at him, and asked, "Want to what?"

"I don't know." He kicked at the ground. "It's just been hard all around."

"Yeah," I whispered. I wiped fresh tears away.

"I wish I could do something to help you." The pain in his expression was genuine, and it only made me feel worse.

"You just did."

"I mean... More than that. With everything."

"You are. You found out about Tom's history. And that Ray's tires match the ones at Hugo's campsite. That's a huge step forward."

"What about all this?" He waved his hand around to indicate the campground.

"Let's hope this murder doesn't set us back."

"And what about... us?" He shoved his hands into his jeans' pockets and looked down. "We don't hang out anymore. We don't talk."

"I know." What else could I say? He knew why. "I'm sorry. I have too much to do today."

"You need to sleep."

"The world officials are coming. I have to meet with them and show them around and tell them about the murder investigation."

"I can do that. You need sleep, Thea. You look dead on your feet."

"Thanks a lot." I wiped away another tear and felt the damn close to bursting.

"I just mean, you won't be good to anyone if you can't even think straight."

"Or what you mean is, you want to tell the officials your side of the story without interference."

He held his hands up in a surrender position. "By my 'story,' do you mean that I'm *not* the killer? Is that different than what you would tell them?"

I sighed. "No."

"They're cornhole officials. They're not coming to investigate the murder, nor do they have any authority to do anything about it."

When I didn't respond, his face fell into a cold stare. "Tell me the truth, Thea. Are you convinced that I killed Hugo?"

I shook my head and fresh tears fell. "I'm only convinced that I do need sleep. You're right." I wiped my cheeks. "If you're sure you don't mind."

"I'm sure."

I turned away, calling again for Gar. Inside, the kittens still milled around in the blanket pile, meowing pitifully as they searched for their missing mother.

I found the bottle and filled it with milk this time. The orange kitten eagerly drank, and when I tried to feed the others, he came back wanting more. When they'd finished the bottle and settled in to snooze, I laid down on the couch and cried myself to sleep.

Chapter 10

When I woke from my nap, I felt refreshed but disoriented. The light had moved in the hours of the early morning, and I had the feeling that I'd missed too much. I grabbed my walkie.

"Hey," I said to Nolan.

There was a pause before he answered, "You get some rest?"

"Yeah. How's it going with the officials?"

"Good," he said. "They want to talk to you at some point."

"Alright. I'll be down soon."

I fed the kittens and headed down to the front of the campground with Gar. I found Nolan in my office with the officials, looking over papers spread across my desk.

Nolan saw me first and Gar went to him to get petted. "Hey Thea."

A man and woman, both dressed in business attire, turned toward me. They wore serious expressions and badges on their jacket pockets with their photo and the words, "Worldwide Cornhole Organization Official" underneath.

"Hi, I'm Thea Pagoni, the owner."

"Susan." She stuck her hand out and I shook it.

"I'm Eric." I shook his hand as well.

"We were just going over some of the event details," Nolan explained.

"We also wanted to ask you a few questions," Susan said.

"Of course. Anything to help," I said.

"These two." Eric shook his head. "Brian and Hugo had issues last year at regionals. Brian failed to pitch the bag within 15 seconds and Hugo called it. Brian contested, but in the end, the call held and he was eliminated. He let everyone in the organization know how much he despised Hugo."

"I wouldn't put it past him to cheat," Susan added. "And I wouldn't be surprised if he was involved in this murder somehow."

"That's what we've been trying to figure out," I said, then added, "The police are investigating several suspects. We try to help them as much as we can, but there isn't much proof, and what we have doesn't point to one person."

"What can you tell us about Ray Kline or Juan Vega?" Eric asked. "We want as much information about them as possible to get an idea of what happened during the competition."

"Ray and Brian have been suspected of conspiring, and Juan is known to hate them both," Susan said.

I nodded. "Ray and Brian are suspects for the murder. We found Ray's tire tracks at Hugo's campsite. He was also heard saying he hated Hugo and that he should be the head official, not the assistant." The reminder of Ray's tracks spiked my anxiety. I had to go talk to him again and see if I could get more from him. "Juan has proven to be violent and disgruntled, so we might need to add him as a person of interest, and we have two suspects who aren't cornhole players."

"Who are they?" Eric asked. "Outsiders could have aided the players in a cheating scheme as well."

I glanced at Nolan and looked quickly away. "A camper who got into an argument with Hugo and was seen using the murder method, and, uhh, the man who found the body."

"I thought you found the body," Eric said to Nolan.

Nolan nodded.

"Oh." Eric shot a quick look at Susan, who shrugged.

"Who do you think is most likely the killer?" Susan asked me.

"I guess whoever had the most to gain. Ray? Brian? Do you think the murder and cheating are connected?"

"They could be," she said. "We want to get whatever information we can on the murder to help us figure that out."

"You don't think the camper or... Nolan were involved?" Eric asked.

I shook my head.

"And what about you?" Eric asked Nolan. "Who do you think did it?"

"I always thought Tom—the camper—was off," Nolan said. "But something isn't right with that Brian, either."

"Interesting," Susan said. "So, you do think this other camper could be involved?"

"I don't think Tom had anything to do with fixing the competition," Nolan said. "No obvious connections there that I've seen. But he could be involved in the murder."

"Thea?" Curtis asked over the walkie talkie.

"Yes?" I stepped into the main office and walked past Sally.

His words came out slowly. "Saw something up here you might want to know about."

"What's that? Where are you?"

"That Tom Adkins? Saw him attacking a log off the main loop near the swimming beach."

"What? When?"

"Just now. He's still at it."

I called Gar from my office and dashed outside, then ran up to my cabin to get my car, forming my plan. If Hunter and Tom were as inseparable as Samantha claimed, where was Hunter while Tom was out punching logs?

I drove quickly to Tom's site and parked around the bend to be less obvious. Gar walked by my side as I approached site 62. Samantha sat reading by the empty fire ring. She looked up and smiled, then held a finger to her lips and pointed to the tent. Through the front opening, Hunter was visible, napping.

I waved to her and walked for a while, making it seem like I was only passing by, before returning to my car. "So, the boy does nap," I said to Gar as I drove along Walleye Circle. I saw a downed log where Curtis had indicated, but no Tom. I drove slowly back to the office, eyes peeled for him.

When I got to the office, Curtis was on the porch, telling Sally his tale.

"Can you start over?" I asked him. "What did you see?"

"An old, rotted log. That Tom was up there, punching it over and over." Curtis made very slow punching movements. "And he was shouting and grunting. Knuckles looked cut up."

"Did you hear him say anything specific?" I asked.

Sally asked, "Was it scary?"

Curtis looked at her with one eye. "Nothing scares me anymore."

"Wow," she said. "I would have run away if I saw something like that."

Curtis's chest puffed up. I rolled my eyes.

"Did Tom say anything?" I repeated.

"Lots of filthy words."

Hennie appeared out of the woods, riding her four-wheeler toward us.

"Did you say anything to him?" I asked Curtis and waved to Hennie.

"Just warned him that he was on private property and was causing damage. He stopped right quick when he knew I was watching."

"Thanks Curtis."

"Better get back out there." Curtis shuffled to his golf cart and drove off to continue his patrol.

"How you holding up?" Hennie asked.

I caught her up on the latest with the world officials and Tom's outburst. "Tom keeps looking guiltier and guiltier."

Hennie nodded.

"Maybe Nolan is right," I said. "He thought Tom did it from the start."

"Don't you want him to be right?"

"I just don't want him to be guilty." My head and chest felt heavy. "I can't take anything else going wrong in my life."

"Oh, honey," Hennie slung her arm over my shoulders. "That's just how it goes sometimes. But I don't think you need to worry about him. He's a good man. And he's hurting, too. He's lonely and feeling rejected."

I looked at her in surprise. "Feeling rejected?"

"By you."

"Just because I think he could be guilty? The police think that, too. I've been trying to find something to clear him."

"But you've distanced yourself from him."

"What else can I do?"

"Trust him," Hennie suggested.

I shook my head. "Last time I did that, it didn't turn out so good."

"Nolan is not your ex."

"I know," I said, "but if the police haven't been able to clear him, don't you think I need to pay attention to that?"

"I think you need to pay attention to your heart. He's got it bad and so do you."

I scoffed. "He does not."

Hennie put a hand on her hip and cocked her head. "Does so. I heard him talking about it and everything."

"What! Talking to who?"

"Not sure. He was on the phone."

"Then you have no idea what he was actually talking about," I insisted.

"Except I heard him say, 'No, it doesn't look like anything will happen with Thea now.'"

My mouth popped open. "What else did you hear?"

"He said he had been interested and still is. But that he doesn't see how you two can start something after all this murder stuff."

"But—" My mind swirled. He really was interested in me? Had I missed it? "We're just friends. And coworkers."

"He wants it to be more."

I shook my head. "It can't be. And the murder thing is just one more reason."

"When are you going to stop making excuses and just live your life?"

Her words had taken on a sharp tone, and I stepped back. My chest tightened, and I knew I was coming off defensive.

"I don't want to end up in another bad situation, okay? When I married Russell, I never thought he was capable of doing the things he did to me. He turned out to be a completely different person. How do I know Nolan isn't the same way? That I'll fall for him and be lured in and then one day, he'll snap and I'll end up in the hospital."

Hennie let out a slow breath. "Whoa, girl. That's heavy."

I looked away and said nothing. I had to push the whole thing out of my mind so I could stay focused.

After a while Hennie said, "I see your hesitation and don't blame ya, but I have a feeling about Nolan."

"I wish I could trust your instinct when it comes to him. I really do," I said. "But I can't even trust mine."

"I think you know in your heart that he didn't do it."

"I can't trust my heart, either."

"Then what will you do? Keep working with a possible killer?" she asked.

"I'm not going to fire him on suspicion. If the cops take him in, then I'll know. Right now, I'm going to find Tom and see what the deal is. He keeps proving how unpredictable he is."

"Let me at least go with you." Hennie patted her side holster, where her handgun rested. "I got protection."

We walked to Tom's campsite and before we reached it, I could see that he was back from his log-punching escapade.

Hunter appeared to still be sleeping. Tom's wife was cleaning his knuckles.

"Oh, what happened?" I asked.

Tom jumped at my voice. "Oh, hi there." He forced a laugh. "You know, the woods can be dangerous."

"I know. A perfectly innocent log was attacked today."

Tom swallowed hard and put on a strained smile. "Boy, you are vigilant around here. I'm surprised two murders have taken place with the way you're always watching."

"Want to tell me why you were punching the log?" I asked.

"Ouch," Tom said and pulled his hand back.

"Hold still," Samantha said. She scrubbed at his knuckles with an expression that was either anger or determination. Maybe both.

"You know, it is normal to blow off steam," Tom said.

"His therapist recommends it," Samantha added defensively.

"So, you punch logs when you get mad?" I asked.

"Better than punching a person," Tom said. "It helps me avoid becoming violent if I let that rage out in a healthy way."

"Don't seem too healthy for your knuckles." Hennie grunted. "You'll break your hand doing that. Get a punching bag, for criminy sake."

"We have several at home," Samantha said.

"What had you so angry?" I asked.

"I find it a tad distressing to be considered a murderer." Tom glared. "Wouldn't you?"

"Sure, but lots of people have been questioned, and if you're innocent, you have nothing to worry about."

"Maybe." He pressed his lips into a line. "Unless I get framed."

"What makes you think you might be?" I asked.

"That security guy? Nolan? I saw him poking around my campsite. I think he did it and is trying to set me up."

"Nah, he wouldn't do that," Hennie said.

I added, "I think Nolan is trying to find anything he can to clear himself." I noted a hint of my own defensiveness and wondered if that was a sign that deep down, I did trust Nolan.

"Well, this is your campground," Tom said. "So, you better make sure no one does anything stupid."

"I'll do my best." I narrowed my eyes at his threatening tone. "Why are you still here if it's so difficult? The police haven't said you couldn't leave."

"We can't miss all the fun." Sarcasm slipped into Samantha's words. She sighed. "Hunter is having a blast with all the players. He's sleeping with his signed corn bag." She glanced to the tent.

"I'd rather be here to know what I'm dealing with," Tom said. "If Nolan is trying to frame me, I will stop him any way I have to."

I narrowed my eyes again and felt my defensiveness increase. "He is an ex-cop and ex-soldier. I'd be real careful there, if I were you."

Tom swallowed hard as his toughness faded.

"Daddy?" Hunter called out from the tent.

Tom spun and hurried to his son. A moment later, they came back out, Hunter in Tom's arms, rubbing his eyes sleepily.

"If you don't mind," Tom said, "we have some mini golf to play."

CHAPTER 11

Hennie and I walked away from Tom's site, following behind Gar.

"We need to talk to Ray about those tracks," I said. "I've been wanting to talk to him again since I found out."

Hennie nodded, and we continued on to Hook Loop, where the cabins were located. When we got to cabin 2, which was Ray's, we saw that his car was gone. I knew he hadn't checked out since he wasn't allowed to leave until the WCO officials cleared him. I knocked just in case he was there.

When no one answered, we returned to the office. Chaos had erupted while we questioned Tom. Susan and Eric were each talking animatedly on their separate phones while also talking to each other. Papers flew back and forth and the *Official Cornhole Competition Rulebook* sat open on my desk.

I looked to Nolan, and he stepped out of the office, closing the door behind him to talk to Hennie and me. The three of us walked out to the front porch for privacy.

"They found weighted bags in Brian's possession," Nolan explained. "He's been disqualified. And when they questioned him about it, he confessed that Ray helped him switch the bags. So, Ray is done, too."

"Wow. Okay," I said. "And we talked to Tom, who thinks you're framing him."

Nolan pulled his eyebrows together. "Okay?"

"He said he saw you looking around his site."

"Yeah. For evidence."

"And that's why I told him you were only looking to clear yourself. But he took that to mean you might clear yourself by making him look guilty."

Nolan shook his head and set his jaw. "There's more," he went on. "The second-place winner should have taken Brian's place, but since Juan assaulted Brian, he's been disqualified, too. The third-place winner is now the champion. Rose Gilbert, 76, of Branson. I think she's a clear candidate for the murder. She might've taken Hugo out and then orchestrated this whole thing to win."

I raised an eyebrow. "Seriously? You think a 76-year-old woman did all that?"

"Of course not. But I do think she has the hots for Curtis. She likes his uniform."

"What uniform? His Cedar Fish shirt?"

Most days, Curtis wore his campground t-shirt with jeans or khakis, like Nolan and I did. Sally was the only who preferred to wear her personal attire—usually a sundress—every day. She told me it made her feel prettier and more professional, so I'd allowed it. I only bought the t-shirts because they were cheap and it meant I didn't have to think about what I wore every day.

Nolan chuckled. "You'll see. Ever since he caught Tom with the log, Curtis has been taking this new role very seriously. Seems you don't even need me."

"Of course I do," I blurted without thinking.

He tilted his head and looked amused by my reaction. "Didn't think you'd feel that way about a murder suspect."

I sucked in a breath and said, "Well, if Brian just got disqualified and Ray just got fired, who will stop them from flipping out again and killing someone else? Or each other. Are the officials safe?"

"I'll make sure of it."

"See, that's what I need you for," I said.

He nodded slowly. "But that's also the problem, isn't it?"

"What do you mean?"

"And that's my cue to skedaddle," Hennie said.

I jumped when she spoke. I'd been so wrapped up in my conversation with Nolan that I'd forgotten she was standing behind me. "You don't have to."

"Got some things that need tending to anyhow. So long as you're holding up, I'll let you two have at it."

"We're not—" I started, but she held up a hand.

"Play nice." She winked and turned to leave.

I glanced around us to see what else I'd been missing. The closest campers were at the wildlife area, several hundred feet away. I reluctantly met Nolan's gaze.

"I'm the muscle," he said. "You like that when it's protecting you, but you're also afraid of it."

I opened my mouth, but couldn't argue.

He looked down at his boot. "I don't blame you. What your ex-husband did was... horrifying." He shook his head. "Domestic calls were always the worst. I've seen some terrible things."

The mention of it alone made me go cold. It didn't help that one of Nolan's eyes was still circled in purple bruises from the fight with Brian and Juan. The swelling had gone down, but it made him appear more menacing than usual.

"What do you know about that?" I asked. When he didn't say anything, the answer came to me. "You looked me up."

"Of course. Are you telling me that you didn't run a background check or a Google search on someone you hired to do security?"

My throat thickened. "It was kinda nuts when I hired you, remember? I didn't have time for all that."

"And since then?"

"I did," I admitted. "I searched online. I didn't like what I found."

He nodded in understanding and pressed his lips together, refusing to look at me. "So, then you know."

"Why didn't you tell me you got fired?"

"Why didn't you tell me your ex assaulted you?"

I picked at the skin around my thumb, wishing I had ice to crunch instead. "I didn't want to come off as weak and stupid."

"You didn't. But there you go."

"There what goes?"

"That's why I didn't tell you," he said. "I didn't want to come off as weak and stupid, either."

"Oh."

Our eyes finally met, and we stared at each other for a tense moment. A strange mix of empathy, anxiety, vulnerability, and longing tangled through my chest. Why did things have to feel so complicated?

"If you need time to see the real me, fine." His tone was soft and almost pleading. "But once you decide, don't change your mind later. I don't want to be playing games."

I owed him that much. "I will."

I struggled to swallow. The real fear that Nolan wasn't who he claimed to be haunted me. But a new fear crept in. What if he really was one of the good ones and my insecurity pushed him away?

"I need to get some air." I sucked in a shaky breath and reached down to sink my fingers into Gar's fur.

"I'll hold down the fort."

Gar and I walked away, leaving Nolan standing on the office porch.

I headed in the direction opposite of Tom's, Brian's, and Hugo's sites. When I saw the entrance of the east trail, I decided to make a short hike of it.

The five-mile trail was our longest, but I only needed to go far enough to clear my mind. I thought a lot about Nolan and what he'd said as I stepped over rocks and Gar pounced on the leaves and critters.

Nolan had figured out why I was fearful of him. Instead of using it against me or seeing me as weak like I thought he might, he was understanding. I wasn't sure what to think or feel about that. I'd never had someone see me so easily. And I'd never had so many broken parts to hide.

The problem was, I couldn't see Nolan easily at all. Between his violent and aggressive past careers and the evidence that made him look guilty of murder, it seemed obvious who he should be on paper. But I had known Nolan for months now, worked with him closely every day, gotten to know him, and been through difficult situations with him. The past I knew existed didn't match the Nolan I knew today. When he seemed like two different people, how could I ever know when I'd seen the real him?

I left the trail, and Gar ran ahead of me in the direction of the pavilion. I followed rather than call him back. When we neared the pavilion, I saw a couple making out at one of the picnic tables. I thought back to the story I'd told Nolan of my first kiss, and how it'd been at a picnic table in that pavilion.

The memory made me miss Nolan. I'd gotten used to walking the grounds with him and talking to him about everything from murder suspects to complaining campers. Cedar Fish felt empty without his friendship.

As we neared the pavilion, Gar barked out a hello. The couple paused and turned to us. I almost burst out laughing.

Curtis looked up at me like a teenager caught parking. Red lipstick was smeared around his mouth. Rose blushed and looked down, covering her mouth to hide her giggles. Curtis's uniform was another sight. He'd been a Navy man in his youth. Apparently, he hadn't changed much physically—his service uniform fit him just fine. I had to admit, it did make him look younger, fitter, sharper, and more handsome. I thought he was even standing straighter.

Curtis dipped his pointed hat to me. "Miss Thea."

I nodded back, still holding in my laughter, and continued on my way. The second I was out of sight, I took out my phone to text Nolan what I'd just seen. But before I typed a word, I put my phone away. Uncertainty settled in my stomach like a rock. I couldn't count on Nolan's friendship right now, no matter how badly I wanted things to go back to how they'd been. I let out a long sigh that didn't relieve the heaviness in my chest.

Going home that night didn't make me feel much better. I fed the kittens and felt Dill's absence. I still had the untouched pan of baklava in my refrigerator. And I still didn't know who had killed Hugo.

It was interesting, though, that the world officials had found weighted corn bags in Brian's campsite. If I had found them, would I have even known? Probably not. What other clues might I be missing? Nolan had searched Tom's campsite for something. I should be looking for more evidence, too.

The next morning, I got my chance. Curtis had called to tell me that he'd seen Ray packing up his things. Once the competition ended, Ray had only stayed because the officials ordered him to. Since the investigation was closed and he'd been fired, he had no reason to stick around. It was my last chance. I hurried over to his cabin with Gar and kept my ears and eyes peeled.

Ray stormed out of the cabin, a bag slung over one shoulder, and almost tripped in his haste.

"Hey there." I waved.

He looked over and shoved his bag into his trunk with force. "Oh," he said dramatically. "Is there *another* problem?"

"Not at all. I just wanted to see how you were before you left. I heard what the officials did."

"It was just awful!" He threw his hands up, let out a cry of frustration, and stormed back inside the cabin. He returned a moment later with another bag, struggling to carry it in his distress.

Ray shoved the bag into the trunk, then stood to face me with hands on his hips. Tears sat in his eyes and his voice sounded unsteady. "It was just so terrible. I know I shouldn't have helped Brian, but I hated Hugo, too! And we had a deal. If I helped Brian, he would do all he could to discredit Hugo and make sure I became the head regional official. Wouldn't you do almost anything to advance in your dream career?"

I thought back to the long hours of law school, the years of sizable student-loan payments, the stress of being a partner. I'd spent a lot of years dedicated to the law. "I can understand that. I was a lawyer in another life."

"Well," he said with surprise. "You just do it all, Miss Thea, don't you?"

"I gave it up, though, when it wasn't worth it anymore. Maybe this will be a fresh start for you. You could try something else you love."

"But cornhole is my whole world! I don't have anything else, and now that I'm banned for life, I have nothing! Nothing!" He covered his face and broke into sobs.

"I'm sorry. That's really hard, but I bet you can think of something. What have you always dreamed of being?"

"A worldwide cornhole official so I can travel the globe and watch cornhole."

I scrunched my face in thought. "Well, you still could. You're not banned from watching the games, only from participating in them. You could be a travel writer and review the games and players. Or a gossip blogger, revealing the scandals of the cornhole world. Maybe you could even coach young players. I know a little boy who would love to take lessons."

Ray paused. "Gossip? I do like the sound of that."

"There you go. Put all this behind you and move on." Assuming he wasn't the murderer, of course, but I didn't think I needed to mention that.

"Oh, that Brian Melton." Ray tsked and shook his head. "I never should have gotten involved with him. I knew better, but my greed blinded me."

"It does that to us all."

He tossed his hands up again and went back into the cabin. While he was inside, I looked around. I glanced into his trunk and noticed a thick hose stuffed in the back. Thick enough to fit around an exhaust pipe.

I took several photos: some that showed the whole car with the hose in the trunk and many closeups of the hose. I even moved a bag out of the way to get better shots. When Ray came out again, I quickly returned my phone to my pocket.

"Well, despite everything that happened, I hope you enjoyed your time at Cedar Fish Campground," I said.

"If it weren't for all the bugs, it would be just lovely. For a campground, it's rather nice. Even if quite dirty." He pulled his lips back in disgust and shivered.

"Great. Well, come back and visit us again." I waved and walked away.

I didn't know much about hoses, but I thought Nolan would know something. Maybe this could clear him.

I called on the walkie, "Where are you?"

"Pool."

"Wait until you see what I just took pictures of."

When we reached the pool, Gar dashed toward Nolan and received a hearty greeting. I, on the other hand, received a head nod and a glance.

I pulled up the photos. "I saw this in Ray's trunk while he was packing up."

Nolan looked closely and his eyes widened. "This could actually be something."

"That's what I thought."

He inspected it for some time. "There's duct tape residue on the ends."

"Really?" I leaned closer to look over his shoulder. The closeness felt too intimate, though, and I backed away. "Would that be considered the murder weapon?"

"Not exactly, but it's evidence. The police will want to see this. They might arrest Ray."

I gasped. "Well, he's getting ready to leave. I'm calling them."

We walked into the main office, where Sally was busy sweeping the store aisles. We waved hello and continued into my private office. I picked up the phone and called Officer Randall.

"I have something you'll want to see," I told him when he got on the line.

"What's this in relation to?"

"The murder case. I found a hose in the trunk of one of the suspects—Ray Kline."

"That right?" I heard papers flipping in the background.

"I took photos of it, but Ray is packing up to leave right now, so you might want to get here fast."

"Uh huh..." He still sounded distracted.

"I'm thinking there's a good chance this hose was used to put the deadly exhaust into the air mattress? You know, how Hugo Menendez was killed?"

The papers stopped. "Huh. Well, I guess we'll be there as soon as we can."

"Okay, great."

I hung up and shook my head. "I'm still not sure he knew what I meant."

"Let me see the crime-scene photos again," Nolan said. I scrolled to them and he looked for a long while.

"Can't believe I missed that." He enlarged the photo and pointed to a bit of tape residue around the valve of the air mattress. I guess the hose wasn't a tight fit on either end. He needed tape to make it all work."

"I wouldn't have thought Ray was so resourceful. That explains his tire tracks, too." I let out a sigh of relief. "This should be the end of it, right? He's guilty."

My heart wanted desperately to know Nolan was innocent. To know, without a doubt, that whatever was in his past was no longer a part of his life.

"Wait a minute." As he flicked through the photos, his expression grew harder. He shook his head and cursed under his breath.

"What?"

"This car?" He pointed to Ray's white car. "It's a LEAF."

"Uhh, no it's a car..."

He rolled his eyes and pointed harder at the car's model name on the back bumper. "It's a Nissan LEAF. It's electric. It doesn't have toxic exhaust."

"No, that's..." I looked more closely at the car and saw the little "Zero Emission" logo on the back. "How is this even possible!"

"He could have borrowed a car."

"But his tire tracks were at the scene. We didn't find any others."

Nolan rubbed his forehead and cursed again. "I thought we had him."

"We still might. I mean, how will he explain the hose? That makes him at least an accessory, doesn't it?"

"Maybe." Nolan slumped into one of the folding chairs.

The outer office door opened, and I glanced out to see who walked in.

"Ray," I whispered to Nolan and went to the front counter. "Ready to check out?"

"Yes," he said emphatically.

I wondered if I should try to stall him until the cops arrived.

"I hope everything was okay with your stay." I took my time flipping through the filing cabinet to pull out his check-in form. Luckily, our extremely outdated system lent itself to taking up time.

"Well, you know about my issues already." He waved a hand at me. "Last year it was at a hotel. Much better. But this was as nice as could be expected."

"Especially considering the circumstances."

He blew a breath up to his hair, then ran his fingers through it. "It has been a whirlwind, that's for sure. The instant I think I've finally succeeded, it all comes crashing down." He let out a tiny hiccup of a sob and fanned his eyes.

I patted his hand and laid his form on the counter. "Have you thought anymore about what you'll do now?"

"Well, let me tell you that your gossip idea was just divine. I already have the name and website." He waved his palm in an arc as if seeing the name on a billboard or in lights. "Shut Your Cornhole dot com."

I nodded. "Nice."

I glanced at my watch. The cops might arrive soon. If they'd taken me seriously and headed toward us right away. Or it could be hours before they showed up. Time to take things into my own hands.

"I noticed your car earlier," I said. "Does it really have zero emissions?"

"Oh, yes. I would never want to contribute to all the pollution in this world. It's bad enough. Besides, I can't *stand* that smell." He stuck his tongue out in disgust.

"I didn't even know they made cars like that."

"You should look into one. Electric is the wave of the future."

"Did Hugo like your car?"

Ray rolled his eyes. "What did Hugo like besides being a jerk?"

I chuckled. "Right. Did you drive around the campground a lot? White must be hard to keep clean."

"Well, I drove when I had to be somewhere. You wouldn't expect me to walk all the way to the cornhole courts, would you?"

"I guess that is far from the cabins," I said. "I'm so used to walking everywhere, I don't notice."

I glanced over at Nolan and he gave a slight shrug.

I finished the transaction and handed Ray his receipt. "You're all set."

"Thank you, and good luck. I hope they catch that horrible killer soon. Not that Hugo didn't have it coming." He walked away, waving his fingers at us.

When the door shut, I asked Nolan, "You don't think we should have delayed him more?"

He shook his head. "He didn't do it. Randall will probably just take your photos and a statement. If they question Ray about it, it won't be until they've had time to look into it."

"So, back to square one?"
Nolan nodded sadly.

CHAPTER 12

Officer Randall eventually waddled into the campground office with Longshore behind him. I didn't
mind Randall as much, and sometimes he slipped up
and gave me information he shouldn't. But Longshore
was a slimy jerk and didn't seem to like me any more
than I liked him.

"We can head to the rec hall," I told them, nodding
to Sally on my way out. My office was too tiny to fit three
people comfortably, and I only had two chairs. There were
great plans in my mind for the rec hall, but most days it sat
empty and useless.

Gar jumped at the chance to be outside and bounded
ahead of me for a few quick jolts back and forth across the
lawn. I propped the wooden rec hall door open and sat at
one of the picnic tables.

"Officer Randall tells me you found evidence for the murder case," Longshore said.

I nodded and scrolled to the photo on my phone. "I saw this hose in Ray's trunk when he was packing up." I didn't need to point out that we now knew it couldn't be him because of his electric car.

Longshore squinted over my phone and narrowed his eyes. "Do you know where Ray is now?"

"He checked out. I told you guys that when I first called in. I have his address on the check-in form, if you want it."

"We already have that," Randall said.

"Do you have reason to suspect anyone besides Ray?" Longshore asked.

"Sure. I think Tom Adkins or Brian Melton could be guilty. Maybe Juan Vega? He was in that fight with Brian. The same people I thought you were looking into."

Randall shook his head. "We've ruled Juan out."

"What about Nolan Cade?" Longshore asked.

I pulled in a slow breath. I'd been asking myself that question for days now. "What about him?"

"He's here today?"

I nodded. "He lives here, so he's usually here."

Longshore made a note in his notepad. "Good to know. What's he... like? Does he get angry often on the job? Is he good with the campers and animals?"

If they were looking into Nolan's character, that wasn't a good sign. "He's a very calm and down-to-earth person. Hugo was difficult to work with, yet Nolan did what he had to and still managed to stay cool and civil. He doesn't interact too much with the campers, but when he does, it's always good. Animals adore Nolan. I think my dog likes him better than me."

I looked over at Gar, who had curled up on the cool cement floor near the door.

Longshore finished writing and looked at me sideways. "And you have found evidence that says he's guilty and nothing that says he's not?"

I hesitated but had to nod in the end.

Longshore tapped his pen against the pad and looked to Randall.

"How's the evidence on Brian and Tom?" I asked.

"There's not much of it," Randall said.

"I think we'll need to take a look around again," Longshore said.

"Sure."

We left the rec hall, and I stood by the front gate while they got in their cruiser. I walkied to Nolan, "Longshore and Randall are driving through, looking around."

"Thanks for the heads up."

The car pulled to the gate, and I swiped my shiny new key card to open it and let them through. I waved as they drove by and then saw Brian turn into the office parking lot. He must be checking out.

I hurried back inside so I could be at the front counter when he came in. I told Sally, "I got the counter. Could you straighten the aisles and note anything that's getting low?"

She nodded and set off into the store part of the building as Brian walked in the front door.

"Hi there. Checking out?"

"No, actually." He leaned on the counter and didn't look up at my eyes.

What was with this guy? I crossed my arms over my chest and took a step back. "What can I do for you?"

"I was hoping you could point me to the nearest town where there might be some action." He stood up and still insisted on gawking at my chest.

"What sort of action?" Was he asking where he could get laid?

"Slots, cards, whatever."

"Oh, there's not a casino anywhere around here. Probably St. Louis is the closest. That's hours away."

"Gotta be something local. There always is." He leaned on the counter with one elbow.

"Not that I know of. Sorry. Rollie's down the street has a bar, and there are some bars in Branson, if you want to ask around there."

"That's more like it. In fact, why don't you meet me at one of those bars tonight?" His mouth crept into a smile.

"I have to work," I lied. Was he for real? "After being disqualified for cheating, do you really think you should be out gambling and drinking? The police are still looking at you as a suspect for Hugo's murder."

Brian's smile vanished and he stiffened. "What do you mean?"

"I mean, they think you could have killed Hugo and are looking for evidence."

"Well, there isn't any." His tone was defensive and his eyes hardened. "What have you heard?"

Brian had said himself that people could be pushed to do things. Maybe if I got him upset, he would let some piece of information slip.

"Not much," I said. "But getting in that fight with Juan and getting caught cheating in a major competition doesn't make you look more innocent. Take some advice from a former lawyer. You want to keep your nose clean right now. There's plenty making you look bad."

"Look bad? Hey, I'm still a champion!" He jabbed his finger into his own chest. "They can take my title, but they can't change that! I deserve to win. I am a winner. There's no evidence saying I killed Hugo. The police know that."

"That doesn't stop them from looking for it. I'll tell you a secret piece of advice." I even leaned in slightly and dropped my voice to sound more conspiratorial. "If you know who did it or if you want to confess, the police will always make a deal with you. And it'll be far better than what you get if they catch you, trust me."

He glared at me and pulled his lips into a snarl. "I'm not giving them anything."

"Do you have something they would want to know?"

"I gotta get out of here. Which way is Branson?"

I pointed in a general northwest direction. "Most people take 76 to get there."

He nodded once, then took a final stare at my breasts before turning on his heel and storming out.

Apparently I'd succeed in riling him up, though it hadn't gotten me much. I thought he reacted too defensively, but that alone didn't point to guilt.

I returned to my office, where I spent the rest of the day. Having Curtis out doing patrols meant I got a better bang for my employment buck, but it also meant Sally had zero help at the registration counter that doubled as the store cash register. I was glad to see the campground filling up, but more campers meant more work, and I couldn't afford to grow my staff.

I'd gotten into the habit of having the security cameras displaying all the time so that whoever was in the office could view the lot of them at a glance. Every so often, I looked over and made sure things seemed on the up and up.

Later that evening, I sat in my office finishing things I hadn't gotten to during the day, like the ad to sell my car. When the cameras switched from normal mode to their nighttime black and white mode, the shift caught my attention. I let my gaze move from camera to camera. In the top, right corner was the view that showed part of the north trail. After what happened there a few months ago, I wanted to be sure we had a good shot of the cliff at the top of Ribbit Rock.

Someone was there. A man, throwing things over the edge of the cliff. I clicked to bring the image up large enough to fill the screen. It was Tom Adkins. I snatched my phone and walkie talkie and headed for the door.

"Gar, let's go check this out." He followed eagerly.

We hurried our way to the north trail and down the mile or so it took to get to Ribbit Rock. When we grew closer, the clatter of rocks cascading down the cliff mixed with grunts of anger.

I hesitated before moving closer. I should probably call Nolan, but I was already there. And Tom wasn't doing anything too terrible, but I still couldn't let him keep throwing rocks. He could hurt someone or destroy something. It was also rather loud and he was disturbing the wildlife.

"Hey Tom, what's going on?" I asked.

He let out a holler of surprise and stopped, hand in mid-air, holding a large rock. "You! What do you want?" He threw the rock with all his might and shouted as it fell.

"I want to know what you're doing. It seems that you have an awful lot of anger to deal with. Much more than you let on."

He growled in frustration and this time, when he let the rock go, it came flying at my head.

"Hey!" I jumped out of the way.

"Leave me alone!" He picked up a handful of smaller stones and kept throwing at me.

"Stop throwing rocks!" I held my hands up to protect my head and face. Gar barked, and I held him back to avoid being hit.

"I am not a violent person!" Tom hurled a bigger rock over the edge of the cliff. "Why can't you see that?"

"Maybe because you keep doing violent things!" I scrunched behind a tree and kept Gar at my side. While hunkered down, I pulled my phone from my pocket and sent a covert text to Nolan: "Tom has flipped at Ribbit Rock. Need you NOW!"

"What has you so upset?" I dodged another rock.

"These cops keep asking questions. You keep asking questions. My wife is asking questions. Everyone thinks I killed someone! I wouldn't do that!" He threw several rocks quickly, creating a chaotic stone trickle.

"Don't you want them to find the guy who killed Hugo?" I asked.

"Yeah, but that's not me! Do I look like a killer?"

Tom's hair stuck out in various directions, and his clothing appeared dirty and disheveled. He looked a bit out of his mind at the moment and very possibly like a killer.

"This isn't helping your case," I said. "Calm down and prove to everyone that you're not violent. This is making you look guilty."

He tugged on his hair and shouted up at the darkening sky, "I've changed!"

"Hey there, buddy." Nolan's strong voice broke into the din. Just knowing he was close comforted me.

Tom snapped his head to Nolan. "You. You're just as bad as her! I know you're trying to frame me."

"No one is doing any such thing." Nolan inched closer to Tom. "Now, how about you put down the rocks?"

"This is how I get out my frustration." Tom hurled two more rocks over the cliff.

"That may be," Nolan said. "But you're on private property, so unless the owner says you can, this isn't the way to get rid of your anger."

Tom's torso ballooned and deflated. He clutched the rocks and glared at Nolan. "And what are you going to do?"

"Well." Nolan reached behind his back to pull out his handgun, aiming it upward instead of at Tom. "I'll start by calling the police to arrest you. If you don't settle down before they get here, I'll have to subdue you myself. I don't think you want to have to explain to your wife and son that you got arrested for disorderly conduct and destruction of property."

Tom let the rocks fall from his hands.

"What if Hunter wakes up and you're not there?" I said. "You better get back to your family."

Tom nodded and looked defeated. He trudged a few steps forward and asked, "You won't call the cops, will you?"

As much as I'd love to think the police would be a help in this situation, I knew better. "If you go back to your site and get some rest before you leave in the morning, everything will be fine."

Tom hung his head as he walked off.

We waited until he was a good distance ahead of us—out of immediate earshot, but within sight.

"I don't trust him at all," I whispered to Nolan.

"You shouldn't."

"But you just threatened him. What if you're in danger now? What if he throws rocks at you next?"

"Did he throw rocks at you?" Nolan asked.

I nodded. "I ducked them all."

His face fell into a scowl. "Maybe we should call the cops. Crazy dude."

"This makes him more likely to be guilty, right?"

"Not always. You never can tell what will push someone over the edge."

"I guess you know better than me."

"What does that mean?" he snapped.

His anger made a flare of anxiety rise in my chest. "I mean, you've actually killed someone, so you know what it takes. I wouldn't know."

"You do understand that war and police work are different than murder."

"I understand they all involve killing."

He shook his head slowly. "So, that's it? I've killed before, so I must have done it. You'll never see me as anything else."

"I didn't say that. It's just that there is a lot of evidence tying you to the scene, you had motive and opportunity, and since all the obvious leads keep fizzling out... It makes sense that the police are still investigating you."

"It makes sense to you because you're convinced I might be a murderer."

I paused to look at him. "I'm not convinced of anything at this point except that we have nothing that proves you're innocent."

"This is America. It's supposed to be innocent until proven guilty."

I held up a finger. "But when you're investigating a murder, everyone is a suspect until proven innocent. *You* told me that."

He stopped to look me deep in the eyes. He searched there, but what he was hoping to find, I didn't know.

When he said nothing for a long time, I finally blurted, "Just give me something that proves you didn't do it so I know for sure!"

"Proof. That's what it'll take to convince you I am who I say I am?" His hands raised slightly in a surrender position. "At one point, I thought there could be something between us. But if you're so convinced in your heart that I might have killed this guy, then I don't see how anything could ever happen. I would have been fine with not getting romantic because your friendship means that much to me, but I don't know how to even be friends with someone who thinks I'm a murderer, and I definitely can't work for someone who'll always be wondering."

"What are you saying, Nolan?"

He stopped and pinched the bridge of his nose. When he spoke, his eyes were hard. "If knowing me isn't enough proof of my innocence for you, then consider this my two weeks' notice."

"What?" His words collided into each other in my mind and bounced back. "Two weeks' notice? You can't quit."

"You want to keep someone around who might be killing off your campers?"

"Well, no, but when the police—"

"You're really not getting it."

Tom had gotten far ahead of us and when Nolan saw this, he started walking again.

My heart lurched in my chest, but there was little else I could do. I couldn't fully trust him, even if I desperately wanted him to be innocent. I couldn't even blame him for quitting. Were I in his place, I'd have done the same. I'd even had the thought that I maybe should fire him.

But I didn't want him to leave. I didn't want to lose him. The thought of seeing him go twisted my insides painfully. I couldn't allow myself to think about the part where he'd said, "I thought there could be something between us." If I opened that can of worms, I'd never get it closed again.

My cell phone rang and the number on the ID said Outer Branson Police Department. I blew out a breath and answered.

"This is Officer Longshore, calling for Thea Pagoni," he said.

"Hello. What can I do for you?" I slowed my pace to create more distance between Nolan and I.

"Can you tell me if Nolan Cade is on the property at the moment?" he asked.

My heart skipped at the question. "Yes, he is. I'm looking right at him."

"Can you keep him there for a little while?" he asked.

"He's working, so I don't think he's going anywhere."

"I just need you to make sure. Can you do that for me?"

"Uhh..." Something felt ominous about the way he said it.

"We just need to talk to him."

"I'll make sure." I hung up and caught up to Nolan.

He turned to look at me, but said nothing.

"The police are coming," I said. "Not for Tom. They want to talk to you."

"Me?" He looked concerned.

I nodded. "They asked me to make sure you stayed until they got here."

"Damn it!" He kicked the ground.

"What? They just want to talk to you."

"No, I'm being arrested."

I shook my head. "Longshore didn't say anything like that. He just said they had some questions."

"Yeah," Nolan said. "And they will take me down to the station to ask them and then keep me there. They must've decided I'm their prime suspect."

"That can't be it. You're reading too much into it."

"Did you forget I was a cop for ten years? You think I don't know police-speak?"

"We'll see."

He rolled his eyes. "You better call Curtis to follow Tom back to his campsite."

Chapter 13

While Nolan and I waited in the office for the police, I cleared some papers off my desk. That way, they could question him without my stuff getting in the way.

"They're here," Nolan said.

We walked outside to meet them. Officers Longshore and Randall got out of the car. The two of them made up about half of the Outer Branson department. And their numbers had increased recently with the murder investigations.

"Hey there," Nolan said. "Where's Detective Hooley?"

"Back at the station." Randall pulled his belt up over his round stomach.

"We're thinking maybe you'd like to come down and talk to him," Longshore said.

Nolan nodded. "Am I being arrested?"

"Am I holding out handcuffs?" Longshore said.

"See," I whispered to Nolan as he walked by.

I figured he would be gone a few hours and then they'd bring him back. Maybe they found some new evidence and wanted to get his take on it. Maybe it would be the thing that cleared him. I kept telling myself that, but watching Nolan climb into the back of a police cruiser and be taken away made my stomach tighten.

When my phone rang an hour later and it was Nolan, I smiled with relief as I answered. "On your way back so soon?"

"Nope."

"Why not?"

"They arrested me. They're holding me as their prime suspect."

My head spun. His words made little sense. "But, but—they can't do that! There's no evidence to prove you did it!"

"Thea." His words were slow and tired. "You've been the one saying all along how much evidence there is. It's enough to arrest me."

"But—" I blinked across the office store to the display of light-up bracelets and realized in the back of my mind that it was running low. "Can I do anything? I could represent—"

"No."

"If not me, then I can call someone who—"

"I don't need a lawyer. I know my rights and how cops work better than you. I have to go," he said. "I just wanted to let you know that I won't be back tonight."

"Are you okay?"

"Yeah," he said sharply and then hung up with a loud click.

I didn't know what else to do but call Hennie.

She answered with a loud, boisterous voice, shouting over the noise around her. "Hello!"

"Where are you?"

"At the VFW. Come on down!"

"You're all the way in Branson?"

"Yup." She hiccuped and shouted to someone before coming back on the line. "Lots of hotties here for you to check out."

"I have enough man trouble already. Nolan got arrested."

"Well, ain't that something. Guess I'll drink to him!" More shouting and muffled sounds. More laughter.

Hennie must be drunk. She definitely wasn't reacting the way I thought she would. I swallowed hard and said loudly, "I don't know what to do."

"Come out and join us!"

"I'm really not up for all that. I'll talk to you tomorrow. Be safe. Let me know if you need a ride."

"Oh, I'm having me a ride. I'm gonna get me a man for the night!" She said and then cackled.

"Okay, well... Make good choices."

"Whoo wee!"

She hung up. I let out a heavy sigh and looked at Gar. "It's up to you and me. What do you say we get up to no good?"

He stood and wagged his tail in anticipation. I went home and ate grilled cheese and tomato soup, then dressed all in black and took my best flashlight.

I never would have seen the hose in Ray's car if I hadn't gone to his cabin to look around. Nolan had been looking around Tom's site, so he must've been hoping that more evidence existed to clear his name. Now that the competition had ended and the cheating drama had been resolved, Tom and Brian were both leaving tomorrow. This was my last chance.

Dressed for my night of ninja sleuthing, I snoozed on the coach for a few hours. My phone alarm went off at 2 a.m., which seemed like late enough that people would be asleep, but still early enough that I'd get some sleep after.

I had trained Gar to be quiet on command. I held my finger to my lips, and he sat, watching me for instruction.

"Let's go," I whispered.

We walked quickly to Tom's campsite and slowed when we neared. I heard only insects in the immediate vicinity. The coals in his fire ring were black and his tent dark.

I took a good look around the site first. I shined my flashlight over their picnic table, revealing various items— plastic utensils, a roll of paper towels, a blue and green plastic bowl, a box of kids' cereal. I viewed each item, but nothing seemed suspect.

I pulled the long sleeve of my black shirt over my hand and tried the van's door handle as softly as I could. The door opened. I switched the interior light off quickly and used my phone and flashlight to look around and take photos.

I pressed the back hatch lever as gently as possible. It opened with a loud pop. I paused to listen. No sounds of movement from the tent.

I searched the back. Besides an abundance of toys and some of their camping gear, they had nothing that helped me. Not even a roll of duct tape that I could say left the residue on the hose and mattress. I closed the van door and hatch quietly and left Tom's site disgusted and frustrated.

I continued down Walleye Circle to Brian's site. His was much messier. He had a cornhole court set up and had moved the picnic table to make room for it. He'd been celebrating with some beer and a pizza, which was evident from his trash. He'd also had several campfires and had struggled to keep his half-roasted marshmallows from melting all over the ground and one bench of the table. His fire ring was full of burned plates and napkins. Beside his fire ring, sitting in the leaves and dirt, was a roll of silver duct tape. I took a photo, though duct tape was common enough I doubted it would mean much in the end.

I moved closer to Brian's tent. Sitting just beside a lantern was a pair of work boots. They looked similar to Nolan's, and I recalled him saying they were very common. I took a photo anyway, turning them to capture the treads.

Unlike Tom, Brian was not so trusting as to leave his car unlocked. I didn't plan to get into carjacking, so I stuck to shining my light through the windows. Besides some food wrappers and a phone cord, his car was empty. I took a photo of the back of the car, but I was pretty sure that an old Pontiac would have deadly exhaust.

The end of the tailpipe showed smudges that could be duct tape residue. I took photos, and my first instinct was to show Nolan. When I remembered where he was, my gut tightened. What if he never came back?

By the time Gar and I headed back toward my cabin, my stomach ached. I walked by Nolan's again in hopes he'd be home, but his camper was dark and quiet. I assumed he'd let me know the second the police cleared him enough to let him go.

I climbed into bed feeling fully grumpy and highly irritated by the fact that murders weren't easier to solve. It felt like the world's hardest game of Clue. Ray had the evidence of the hose and his tire tracks at the scene, but not the car to produce the fatal exhaust. Brian had the car that would kill, and possibly residue on his tailpipe, plus the duct tape and similar boots, but he wasn't the one with the hose. Tom had the rage, history, and murder method, but none of the other evidence. They all had strong motives and weak alibis.

Then there was Nolan. Whose footprints were all over the scene, along with his fingerprints. Nolan, who had found the body, who had been the only one to recognize the problem with inflating something with car exhaust, and who had a thumbtack that might've made the holes in the mattress. He also had plenty of opportunity, plenty of motive, not to mention a violent past and, unlike Tom, had admitted to killing multiple people.

The suspects would be gone tomorrow and Nolan was in jail. My time was up. It looked like the murder had been solved after all, and Nolan had done it. I tried to make things line up in my mind, to picture him driving his truck to Hugo's site and filling the air-mattress. To see him taking the tack from the office corkboard and then sticking multiple holes in the mattress to make it leak.

I turned over and stared across my bedroom. My heart tumbled between the Nolan I knew and this other Nolan I pictured—Nolan the murderer. I couldn't resolve the two. The Nolan I knew was *not* a killer.

Either the police were wrong about him or I was. I forced my eyes closed, hoping more desperately than I ever had in my life that I was right.

CHAPTER 14

My head felt hot with exhaustion when my alarm went off. I'd gotten maybe four hours of sleep.

I made extra strong coffee and did a few jumping jacks to wake up. I took a cool shower and remembered, yet again, that I still needed to have Nolan look at my bathroom and tell me why the water ran brown sometimes. Thinking of Nolan scrubbed away the sleepy-safe haze and brought back all the pain of the day before.

As I toweled off my hair, my phone dinged with a text.

"On my way back," from Nolan.

My heart skipped. They'd cleared him. Hope and joy surged within me.

I sent back, "I knew they would clear you!" and got dressed with a bounce in my step, suddenly feeling energetic.

I made coffee and poured it into two travel mugs, then went to sit on the office porch so I could be there when Nolan got back. A few minutes later, a cruiser pulled up, let him out, and took off again.

I jumped up and grinned, handing the mug out to him. He took it, but shook his head and gave me a weary look. "You misunderstood."

"About?"

"They didn't clear me. I'm out on bail."

The world around me crashed. I sat hard on the swing, and when it moved under me, I almost lost my protein-bar breakfast.

"Then we have to get you a criminal lawyer," I said. "I know plenty of great ones."

He stood in front of me, his whole body sagging with the weight of his exhaustion. Several minutes passed in silence.

"I don't know how long I have," he finally said, "so, why don't you make a list of the most important things you want me to do, and I'll do as much as I can before I..."

I nodded and he walked away slowly. I stumbled into the office and only then realized Gar hadn't followed me. I walked back outside to find him and saw him off in the distance, walking beside Nolan, who had his head down.

I returned to my desk. The photos I'd taken last night were open on my laptop screen, and I scrolled through them numbly. In my searching last night, I hadn't found anything useful. I stared at the thumbtack photo. Maybe it really had fallen off the corkboard and Nolan stepped on it, like he'd claimed. Would a jury buy that when I hadn't? I brought up the photos of Nolan's boots and the crime scene shoe print, then opened the photo of Brian's boots, too. I searched for something in the muddy shoe print that could look like a tack or a hole left behind from one. The prints in Hugo's tent weren't sharp enough to pick up a tiny dot, and nothing so round and smooth as a tack's head seemed to have interrupted the pattern. I next searched the photo of Brian's boots and noticed a sizable gash on the right side of his right foot.

My pulse raced as I looked back to the crime scene. I'd noticed a break in the pattern, but thought it had been a wrinkle in the tent or that some debris had interrupted the print. I looked closer and let out a sharp gasp when I saw that not just one, but two of the shoe prints contained the same gash as Brian's boots.

I printed all three photos. I measured and used a magnifying glass from a kid's bug-collecting kit that I took from the store shelf. Nolan had slightly bigger feet than Brian. When I measured the prints in Hugo's tent, I found two different sizes. Though Nolan's shoe print didn't show something so recognizable as Brian's gash, there were subtle scrapes and dents that could be matched up.

By the end of the hour, I was sure. In the tent were two sets of footprints. Same style of work boot and pattern of tread. Two sizes. One was Nolan's and one was Brian's.

I held the photo of Brian's shoe in my hand with glee. And then I saw something that absolutely made up my mind. In the corner of the tent, near one of Brian's shoe prints, sat a small twig of thorns from a black locust tree.

I picked up my phone with tears in my eyes and dialed Nolan's number.

"It wasn't you!" I shouted. "I know it wasn't you! It was Brian!"

Nolan let out a long sigh. "Did you find some actual evidence or is this you changing your mind again?"

"I found something. I can prove it was Brian. Why don't you sound excited about this?"

"It was a long night. Your call woke me up."

"Oh. I thought you were working today. Sorry. Is Gar still with you?"

"Yes. Give me a few hours and I'll get to it."

"Sure."

I hung up and stared at my phone. It seemed like he didn't even care that I'd finally found something to clear him. My excitement faded and I second guessed myself. I looked back at the photos. No, I was sure. It was Brian.

I picked up the phone again, to call the police this time.

"Who do you think you're calling now?"

I shrieked and dropped my phone. Brian had walked into my private office. He glared and curled his lip threateningly.

"You can't be in here," I said. As if that would stop him.

He closed the door and locked it. Sweat broke out across my skin. I stood up, but there wasn't room to go anywhere in the small space.

"Where is this proof that I killed Hugo?" he growled.

I pointed shakily to the photos on my desk.

He looked them over before tearing them to pieces. "What am I supposed to do now? Just let you live?" Brian squeezed a corn bag tight in his hand.

"You can just turn and walk away. Don't make things worse for yourself."

"Worse?" He slammed the corn bag to the floor. "You're going to give the police proof that I killed Hugo, and you don't think that's bad enough?"

"But if you kill me, that's two murders instead of one." I tried to swallow and inch back. My butt touched the edge of the desk. Of all the times for Gar to spend the day with Nolan.

"Three murders," Brian said. "You're forgetting Nolan."

My heart lurched, for a moment thinking that Nolan was dead. But I had just talked to him seconds ago, I reminded myself. "Nolan didn't do anything."

"He knows I killed Hugo. You just told him." Brian balled his hands into fists, then straightened his fingers and balled them again.

"Maybe you can make a deal," I offered. "Plead temporary insanity. You might only go to jail for a few years. But if you kill three people, you'll probably get the death penalty."

"It's all your fault!" He lunged at me, hands out.

When his fingers closed around my throat, panic suffocated me. But then, something clicked in my brain.

I brought my forearm up and slammed it into his arms to break the hold as I twisted out of his grasp. He half-fell onto the table, and I used the momentum to get behind him and grab his arm.

Brian struggled against me and almost broke free. He jerked harder and landed face-down on the ground. I sat on his legs and held his arms behind his back. He wiggled and kicked at me, but he was small enough that I could hold my position.

I grabbed my phone with one hand, but with the movement of his struggling, it was difficult to dial. The walkie was too far away, at the opposite end of my table desk. When I finally managed to place the call, I moved the phone between my shoulder and ear.

"What?" Nolan mumbled.

"Sorry to disturb your nap, but I have this murderer pinned down in my office right now, and it'd be great if you could help me hold him until the police can get here."

"Say that again?" he muttered sleepily.

"I have Brian! Get over here!" I put the phone down and tightened my hold on Brian. "You should have known better than to attack me. I know karate now."

Brian grunted and jerked his hips up with a forceful motion. It was enough to knock me over, breaking my grip on him.

"No!" I scrambled backward, away from him, under the table desk.

He got down on his knees and came at me again, going for my throat. I frantically swatted at him, forgetting any moves that might help me. Tears streamed down my cheeks and I screamed.

The door slammed open. A moment later, Brian was ripped away from me. Nolan threw him on the ground and pointed his gun in Brian's face. Brian happened to land near the door and rolled through the doorway, jumping to his feet and taking off.

Nolan ran after him and I ran after Nolan, Gar chasing us both. We followed Brian around the office toward my cabin.

"Freeze!" Nolan was close enough to shoot him and trained his gun at Brian's head.

Brian spun, saw Nolan, and dashed to the side. Then he turned and bolted for me.

Before I could assess what was happening, Brian was behind me, his arm tight around my throat.

"I'll kill her!" Brian shouted. "Drop your gun or I will snap her neck!"

Gar barked and growled, tugging at Brian's pant leg to pull him off me. Nolan kept his gun on Brian, but that meant it was also pointed at me.

"You have no idea how to kill someone like that," Nolan said.

"You want to find out?"

Nolan's jaw tightened. "Let go of her."

Gar bit hard into Brian's leg. He yelled in pain and kicked Gar. With a yelp, Gar backed away, his ears flat against his head.

"Maybe I don't want to kill her," Brian said. "Maybe I just want to have some fun and make you watch." He moved his free hand to grab my breast.

Nolan pulled the trigger and Brian dropped to the ground, almost pulling me down with him. His blood was splattered over my left side.

I shuddered and couldn't stop trembling. My knees collapsed and hit the ground. The loudness of the gunshot rang in my ears. The ground tilted and I sat, tightening my arms around my stomach.

Nolan walked over to Brian, his gun still aimed at his head. Brian didn't move. Nolan nudged him with his foot, then stepped closer to me.

He sat beside me and put one arm tight around my shoulders. I stiffened and he let go immediately.

I turned to him, wiped the tears from my eyes, and launched myself at him. Without thinking about it, my arms wrapped around his neck, and I pressed my lips to his.

He didn't kiss me back. Instead, he gently broke my hold on him and moved my arms down, then turned his body away from me.

He tucked a piece of hair behind my ear and said, "We need to call the police."

I nodded and wiped fresh tears. I couldn't begin to process what had just happened with Nolan in the midst of everything else. Had he just... pushed me away?

"Let's go wait for them." He helped me to my feet and supported my weight with his arm around my waist.

When we reached the office, he sat me on the porch swing, kissed the top of my head like he would a child, and stepped away. I couldn't even blink as I watched him take out his phone. He talked to someone, but I was too far away to hear or make sense of anything past the ringing in my ears.

Nolan hung up and came back to me. He studied my eyes for a long moment, then sat beside me. "What did you find that made you sure it was Brian?"

"His shoes. And the thorns."

Nolan disappeared inside for a moment and came back with a bottle of cold water. He handed it to me. "Drink."

I took a few sips and let the coldness wash down my throat, aware suddenly of the few campers milling around, having a perfectly normal day.

"We have to move the—" I jumped to my feet, realizing that at any moment, a camper could happen upon Brian's body, even if it was near enough to my cabin that they wouldn't have a reason to wander that way.

"Don't worry about that. Just sit and drink. I have Curtis taking care of it."

I sat down and stared at the front gate. What needed to happen next? I wasn't even sure what time it was or what day. Shouldn't Sally be in by now?

"Can you explain your evidence?" Nolan asked.

"Brian has the same boots as you. His are smaller and have a gash on the right foot. His prints are in the tent with yours. And by one footprint, there were black locust thorns."

He waited for more explanation.

"Black locust trees used to be all over the campground," I told him. "My grandmother loved the way they looked when they bloomed. But one season, a little boy ate a pod and got very sick. They didn't know the pods were so poisonous. Grandad removed every one of those trees. But one grew back. It's way in the back of Walleye Circle, out of the way, so they left it since we never put kids at a site that far out. Locust trees have very hard, very sharp thorns. That's what Brian used to poke the holes in the mattress, and his was the only site that has access to them."

"Too bad you didn't discover that a day sooner."

"He also confessed to killing Hugo and said he would kill us since we knew."

Nolan put his hand to his face and rubbed his temple.

"You okay?" I asked. "You did just kill someone."

He gritted his teeth and closed his eyes. "I'm fine."

"Why did you get fired from the police force back in St. Louis?"

He didn't open his eyes. "Not now, Thea. Please."

I took a few deep breaths and my brain tried to come back online. "What about the hose in Ray's car? And Brian's tire tracks weren't at Hugo's site."

"I would guess that Brian either borrowed the hose from Ray and returned it or stashed it in Ray's car to frame him or to get rid of the evidence. And the tires? The ground isn't usually soft enough to leave tire tracks. When Ray first got here and drove to Hugo's site, the ground was still wet from all that rain we had, but the day Hugo died, it was likely hard again."

"It all seems so obvious now. I wonder if Brian saw Tom filling the beach ball with exhaust and got the idea."

Nolan shrugged. "Guess I was wrong about Tom."

"No. We needed to eliminate him. He looked really guilty."

The police showed up then, speeding into the campground with their three cruisers, a coroner's car, and an ambulance behind them.

"Now the fun starts," Nolan said.

CHAPTER 15

After the police left, I stayed in bed most of the day and asked Hennie to help out in the office. I couldn't bring myself to face the world yet. I still felt wrung out and raw, and I swear I could still hear the ringing from the gunshot.

When the next morning came, I felt better. The bright sunlight warmed my spirit as I stretched in my bedroom. The weight of the investigation had lifted, as did the worry that Nolan might be a killer. But he'd given his notice, and I didn't know if he intended to go through with quitting. There was also that kiss that left me completely confused. If he was interested, why hadn't he kissed me back? And yet, he didn't make it feel like an outright rejection, either. Not with the tenderness he gave me after.

Gar had moved from the bedroom at some point during my day in bed. He'd been bored, I guessed, and took to playing with the kittens for entertainment. Several items in the cabin were knocked over, including my grandmother's crystal vase. I set it upright on my small kitchen table. Gar's dark, sleeping form made a circle in the middle of the living room floor. And lots of little black spots were dotted all around him.

I walked closer to see what had happened. The three kittens slept snuggled into Gar's stomach. I hadn't even seen them. Sooty paw prints led from the fireplace, around the living room, to where the four amigos slept. The kittens were so covered in soot and ash that they blended into Gar's hair.

I had tried to deny it, but I couldn't. The kittens belonged here. As much as I didn't want to have a bunch of cats to take care of, Cedar Fish was their home. Gar loved having them around, and for an energetic puppy, nothing was better than multiple playmates.

I had been calling them A, B, and C. As I watched them sleep now, dirty from the fireplace, I decided that the grey and white kitten would be Ash, the orange one would be Blaze, and the black and white one would be Coal.

For a moment, things felt complete. But if Nolan left, something would be missing. I had to convince him to stay.

I walked to Nolan's campsite and knocked on his camper door, but he didn't answer. I realized that I had slept late, and he was likely off working. I headed into the office to see if anyone was there. Inside, I found Sally at the register, handing a camper his receipt.

When the camper left, she turned to me. "Are you feeling better today?"

"I am, thanks. Have you seen Curtis or Nolan?"

"Curtis is on patrol. Not sure about Nolan."

"Thanks." I grabbed the walkie and stepped onto the office porch. I took a breath, pressed the button, and asked Nolan, "You busy?"

"Uhh... What do you need?" He sounded distracted.

"Can we talk?"

"I'm at the river mouth."

I took that to be a yes. My heart pounded as I walked down Catfish Lane toward the river. I knew what I wanted to say, but wasn't sure I wanted to hear what he had to say in response.

When Nolan came into sight, the late morning sun rose behind him, creating a silhouette. He stood on the private dock and cast a line into the water. On his head was a hat I'd never seen him wear. My heart jolted. For a moment, it wasn't Nolan. It was Grandad standing there, in his ridiculous hat, fishing at the worst time of day. For him, it was always more about being near the water and away from life for a time than catching anything.

I closed my eyes and let the image settle in my mind. So many memories matched it. So many hours spent by the water, throwing in lines, pulling out fish, talking with Grandad. It felt like he was there with me, which only made me miss him more. He was always so good at reading people. He never would have doubted Nolan. And he'd probably be better at finding murderers than me, too. When I opened my eyes, I wiped away tears and continued my approach. A few minutes later, I reached him.

"Hey there." I stood beside Nolan.

He cast another line into the water. "Hey."

"So..." I twisted my fingers together and forgot everything I'd planned to say.

"Sorry for fishing on the job. I haven't had a day off in ages."

"No, it's fine." He cast his line in again and reeled it back slowly. "I need to be near the water from time to time. Helps me think."

"Is that why you're fishing when you have no chance of catching anything?"

"There's always a chance." He winked and pulled the brim of his hat down.

"Where'd you get the Filson?"

He tapped the brown leather hat. "You like it?"

"It's just like my grandad's. You looked like him standing out here, fishing in the middle of the day like an amateur."

Nolan laughed. "I'd be an amateur if I didn't know better. I'm not trying to catch anything but some peace." He recast his line and faced the water again.

"Should we talk another time?"

"No. Let's get it over with."

I hung my head. "I wanted to apologize."

"For?"

"You know what for. Thinking you killed Hugo."

"And?"

"And for not trusting you."

He nodded and flicked his rod toward the water. "Okay."

"That's it?"

"I accept your apology."

I swallowed hard. "Doesn't seem like it."

"Maybe I just don't get it, Thea. I can see why you might think I did it, especially since I was the only one arrested. But Hugo? You flirted with the guy. And I don't get it."

My face burned with embarrassment. "No, I didn't really."

"Come on." He slid his eyes to me in a stern look.

"It wasn't flirting, I just wanted to make him happy."

He raised an eyebrow as if I'd proven his point.

"I mean, Hugo was difficult from the start," I said, "but that event brought in a ton of money. I wanted to make sure things were perfect so they'd come back next year. And the year after that. We need the business."

"Is that all it was?"

"He also had this weird resemblance to a photo of my grandad, and it was like talking to the younger version of him instead of Hugo. It messed with my head."

Nolan glanced at me again before casting his line. "Hugo and I both look like Grandad?"

I shook my head. "He looked like one photo. You don't so much look like him as act like him. You and Grandad are both strong and quiet, with that calm way of getting things done and putting people at ease. Hugo was the opposite. He was really obnoxious and patronizing. I didn't like how he treated you or Hennie, either."

"Funny. You sure didn't stop it."

"I'm sorry. I should have. But like I said, I didn't want to make him mad enough that he wouldn't come back."

"You really didn't feel anything at all for Hugo?" Nolan looked at me sideways and raised an eyebrow.

"Only revulsion."

He chuckled. "Good."

I swallowed hard and sucked in a breath before I said, "You're the only one that I... want to flirt with."

He finally set his pole down. After a moment of staring at the water, he turned toward me. "I want things to be good between us again. I don't like all this tension."

"Me, either. It's been terrible the last few days."

He nodded and stepped closer. "I don't want you to have doubts about me."

"I don't. I'm so sorry, Nolan. I was just freaked out. I didn't know what to think and I—"

He put a hand to my cheek, and I stopped with my mouth open. I sucked in a trembling breath.

"Do you trust me not to hurt you?"

I gulped. "Mostly. But, it'll take some time for me to see it and really believe it." I closed my eyes and tears fell down my cheeks.

He wiped them away gently with his thumb, and his tenderness made the tears flow harder.

"It's not fair to you, I know," I whispered. "It's Russell's fault." I shook my head. "I never thought a fight over the ice cube tray would lead to him hitting me. I took self-defense classes in college, you know. I thought I would be able to defend myself if anything ever happened. But right there in my own kitchen, he strangled me, and I couldn't do anything to stop it. I really thought I was going to die. And then, when he forced himself on me, I wished I had. Do you know how people look at you, even in the hospital afterward... Like somehow it was my fault. Like I just sat there and let it happen."

He looked deep into my eyes with a pained expression, then pulled me into a tight hug. "I'm sorry that happened to you," he whispered as he stroked my hair.

I continued to cry for several minutes, and his soothing touch softened the severity of the pain.

He pulled back to look at me again. "I would never do that to you."

"I want to believe you."

"You will." His mouth crept into a smile and he leaned down slowly.

I moved toward him, closed my eyes, and waited.

When he pressed his lips to mine, my heart exploded. His hand found the small of my back and his other hand wound behind my neck. I pulled myself closer to him and moved my lips with his.

When the kiss ended after a long while, he touched his forehead to mine and sighed. "Now what?"

"I don't know. I'm so confused. You said you were quitting, and then I kissed you, but you didn't kiss back, and Hennie said you were interested, but I know I messed things up..."

Nolan pulled me into another hug. He kissed me again and shook his head at me. "Thea." He laughed. "I didn't want our first kiss to be beside the body of the guy I just killed for touching you. Didn't seem like the most romantic story to tell our grandkids."

I laughed. "Are you kidding me? It makes you look like a superhero. An epic tale of bravery."

"Do you really believe that?"

I held his gaze for a long moment. "I do. My trust issues run deep, but I'm willing to take a chance, as scary as that is."

"You're not the only one taking a chance or feeling terrified right now."

I soaked in the feeling of his arms around me. Only one thing could make the moment better. "Want to come to my cabin with me?"

Nolan pulled back to look at me with a shocked expression. He tried to speak, but I pressed my lips to his again.

Then I whispered into his ear, "I have an entire, untouched tray of chocolate baklava waiting in my refrigerator and a tub of vanilla ice cream in my freezer."

He let out a soft moan. "And I thought you had something dirty on your mind."

"Oh, I do. When we finish off that baklava, the pan will be so dirty, I'll have to scrub it immediately."

He laughed and took my hand. "Then we better not keep it waiting."

Note from the Author

Thank you so much for reading BREATH OF FATAL AIR. I hope you enjoyed your time with Thea and her crew. I had a blast writing it, and I can't wait to get back there!

Would you consider leaving a review?

Reviews are a huge help to indie authors like me. I'd be grateful if you would give just a few minutes of your time to let others know what you thought of the book. Reviews not only help other readers find the books they're looking for, they help indie authors get seen.

Leave a review:
ZoeyChase.com/BreathOfFatalAir

Thank you!
Zoey Chase

Don't miss the next book in the series!

Fourth of July should have been a blast at Cedar Fish Campground, but another murder has sent Thea's plans up in smoke.

Thea Pagoni is ready to move on from a difficult start to the summer with a huge bash planned for the Fourth of July. But a giant turtle gets in the way—literally— and the closer they get to the event, the grumpier Nolan acts. After Thea's argument with a fireworks vendor leads to threats and tension, having Jerry Bishop, famous purse designer, stay at the campground seems like it could bring some good press... Until he's found face-down and unresponsive in the goat pen.

Another unsolved mystery could ruin the event, and Thea isn't convinced that Jerry's fans and their memorial are good for business. With Nolan and Hennie to help sleuth, along with the rest of the crew at Cedar Fish, Thea sets out to find the latest killer before things blow up in her face.

**Get it here:
ZoeyChase.com/OneBodyShortOfAPicnic**

Read the first chapter of
ONE BODY SHORT
OF A PICNIC
now in this special preview!

To find out more or to purchase, visit:

ZoeyChase.com/OneBodyShortOfAPicnic

My stomach grumbled, making me feel sick in the sticky heat. I checked my watch again—12:20. Gar, my large Newfoundland puppy, looked up at me with a pleading expression. When I didn't get up, he stretched out on the cool cement floor of the vacant rec hall and sighed. My vendor meeting that was supposed to start at 12 should have ended by now, and I should be eating my lunch. I'd started having my meetings in the rec hall, rather than cramming into my tiny office, but sitting here bored and hungry in the heat made me reconsider.

The rec room contained only a few folding tables and chairs. I'd propped both doors open, but there wasn't much of a breeze. My eyes trailed the edges of the room. So much potential. I sighed. We were still in the fixing phase of things at Cedar Fish Campground. But the day would come when I could start remodeling and really do something with the huge, wasted space of the rec hall. I pictured game nights to balance out the bingo, and maybe some crafting events for kids. I could put some pool or ping-pong tables at one end, and it'd be great to add a snack bar. On my most ambitious days, I even saw myself leading a group of campers stretched out on mats, all of us doing yoga in the early morning. But I'd have to learn yoga first.

I picked up my walkie talkie and called to my employee, Sally, in the office. "Hey, have you seen Mr.

Dorsey yet?" When no response came after several seconds, I called back. "Sally? Hello?"

Still nothing. I tried Curtis's channel next. He should be on security patrol and could check on the front of the campground for me. "Curtis, you there?"

When I got no response from him either, my heart rate spiked. I stood and looked out toward the office building next door. Gar jumped up as well, tongue lolling out and ready to play.

"Miss Thea?" Curtis's voice crackled over the airwaves.

I snatched my walkie to my mouth. "Yes, Curtis? I'm here."

"Seems we have a... situation near the front gate."

I gulped. With two recent murders in the campground, that could mean almost anything. "What sort of situation?"

"Maybe you could step out here a moment?"

I grabbed my travel mug of ice from the table and cautiously approached the rec hall door. Gar leapt through it ahead of me and ignored my command to come back. The bright noon sun beat down as I rounded the building.

Curtis, dashing as always in his old military uniform, stood with hands on hips in his usual hunch, inspecting an object on the ground. Sally stood beside him, her wavy red-brown hair almost glowing in the sunlight. They blocked my view of whatever our "situation" was.

Since it didn't seem big enough to be a body, I relaxed and walked closer.

From under a nearby bush, three kitten heads peeked out in a row, also watching with intensity. Gar seemed oblivious to what was going on as he bounded in circles several feet away, batting at flowers and growling at anything that moved.

"What's going on?" I asked.

Curtis and Sally parted and gave me full view of the massive turtle sitting in the middle of the front drive.

I tilted my head at it. "Is that Rollie's turtle?" Rollie's General Store was a mile down the road, but giant turtles didn't seem all too common to me.

Curtis shook his head. "Smaller."

"It's definitely not Rollie's," Sally said. "My boys love to play with that turtle and they find shapes in his shell designs. You know, like how kids do with clouds?" She paused to make sure we followed.

"Cute," I said.

"Well, I know all of their favorite shapes, and this turtle does not have the charging bear or the UFO. Also, this turtle is much... scarier."

She had a point there. Three ridges of spiked shell ran the length of the turtle. The spikes weren't sharp enough to cut or stab, but they made for an intimidating show. The turtle that lived at Rollie's bore similar spiked ridges, but less pronounced.

"So, if it's not the same turtle, do we have any idea where it came from?" I asked.

"Must've come down the river and landed in the lake," Curtis said.

"Will it go back?"

He shrugged.

"Can we move it from the road at least?"

He shook his head slowly. "Would *you* get near that thing? Don't want to lose a hand."

I imagined that, in a showdown between Curtis and the turtle, the turtle would come out faster.

Gar had finished his game of chase with a chipmunk and dashed back to me. When he neared, he must've smelled the turtle. He snarled and approached cautiously until he pressed his side against my legs.

I rubbed his head. "Just stay back, boy."

I stepped closer and bent down, reaching my hand hesitantly toward the middle of the turtle's shell.

"Bad idea," Nolan said.

I jumped at the sudden appearance of my handyman/security guard and fell on my butt. The turtle stuck its head out and hissed at me, its jaws stretching wide before snapping shut again. I scrambled to my feet and backed away. Gar barked, and that made the kittens bolt from their hiding spot. Gar took that as an invitation to chase after them.

Nolan laughed. "That thing could take your finger off in one bite. Were you trying to pet it?"

"No. I was trying to move it out of the way." I kept my eyes on the turtle that looked even more devilish with its pointy head visible.

"That's an alligator snapping turtle and probably weighs 60 pounds," Nolan said.

"If you know so much about it, why don't you go ahead and take care of it?" I patted his shoulder and gave him a curt smile.

"Yes, dear."

A car pulled in and stopped a few feet from us.

"My meeting is finally here anyway," I said. "Can you take Gar?"

Nolan glanced a few feet away where the puppy circled the kittens. He saluted to me and turned to the turtle.

Sally walked back to the office, muttering, "Wait until I tell my boys about this."

Curtis shuffled toward the wildlife pen.

Nolan inspected the turtle, scratching his beard in deep thought. I let my eyes linger a moment on the way his tan Cedar Fish Campground t-shirt stretched tight over his chest and biceps.

With a pleased sigh, I approached the car as the driver's window lowered.

"Hey Mark." I waved. "Sorry, we have a turtle situation. You can just cut through here to get to the parking lot in front of the office."

He nodded and drove where I pointed to the grass between the main entrance drive and the front parking lot.

Mark stepped out of his car wearing a short-sleeved button down and khakis. His blue tie was embroidered with two exploding fireworks in sparkling, metallic thread. The best part was the tiny LED lights that lit from the center of each starburst and blinked their way to the ends of the blast before starting over.

"We'll meet in the rec hall again."

He nodded and followed me past the turtle, Nolan, and Gar.

"You guys all ready for the big holiday?" he asked.

"Getting there," I said. "Lots of little details to finalize. Like this contract."

"Well, this won't take long, and I'll be out of your hair."

I gestured to the rec hall door, and he entered. We sat at the table where my copy of the final contract waited. "I checked everything over, and it all looks good to me."

"Great. And we're set on the initial and final payment amount?"

I slid a check out from under the contract. "I have the first payment right here."

It was more than I should probably spend on one event, but I hoped that the Fourth of July could keep business going. Things had picked up in the last month, but I worried that the second murder would lead to another crash in reservations. We still weren't very profitable, but we'd been slowly increasing. I'd decided to splurge on something huge to draw attention—a live fireworks display, set off right from our very own Dogwood Lake.

"Thank you." Mark took the check, folded it, and slid it into his shirt pocket. "All we need to do is sign."

We signed two copies of the contract, and he shook my hand. "I look forward to your event. It's going to be just as spectacular as you imagined."

"I'm counting on it." I followed him back outside.

Mark walked toward his car, and I returned to Nolan. Gar sat by his side, eyes trained on the turtle.

"You get it figured out?" The turtle stared back at me from the same position it was in before.

Nolan held up his phone, showing several photos of turtles. "I think it's a female."

"Okay, but how do we get her to move?"

"Either wait it out or try to lure her with some fish."

I poured a piece of ice into my mouth and chomped it. "Maybe we can call Enid and see if she has any ideas." I wasn't sure how Rollie's came to have a resident pet turtle, but the store's owner, Enid, was the only person I knew with giant-turtle experience.

Nolan nodded. "Was that the fireworks guy?"

"Yeah. I just signed the final contract."

"You went through with it?" Nolan put his phone in his pocket.

"Uhh, we decided this weeks ago when I gave him the deposit." I crossed my arms. Every time the Fourth of July event came up, Nolan took on some level of grumpiness about it. I'd ignored it, but his attitude grew worse the closer we got to July.

Nolan pressed his lips into a line and shook his head.

"What?" I asked.

"Told you this was a bad idea."

"Having a huge event to draw people to the campground? Why would that be a bad idea?"

"I mean the fireworks part," he explained. "Think about all that could go wrong. Did Mark even look into the ordinances for the area? I haven't seen a permit."

I put my hand on my hip. "That's because the permit stays with the person setting off the fireworks. And a fire crew will be on site. They even agreed to let kids climb on the truck earlier in the day."

Nolan's jaw tightened and he looked away.

"What's the real problem with the fireworks?" I asked.

"With all that's happened this summer, do you really want to risk more campers' safety with something like this? What if there's a fire or an explosion? What if debris falls on someone? I don't think this is a smart idea."

Heat flared up my neck and I took a step back. "Where is all this coming from? Mark is a professional. You were there when he looked at the lake a month ago to make sure there was enough room and that nothing would be in the way. If there is high wind or lightning, he won't do it. It's all in the contract, if you want to read it."

"Forget it." Nolan stalked off.

"What about this turtle?" I called after him.

He didn't turn back around.

I was distracted for a moment by the way his jeans cradled his butt, but my confusion and irritation over his crankiness quickly ruined it. Gar looked up at me as if to ask what Nolan's problem was.

I glanced back at the turtle, and she snapped her jaw in defiance.

"Do you have a problem with fireworks, too?"

She pulled her head into her shell.

"I guess everyone is grumpy today."

If Nolan wouldn't help, I knew I could count on my friend and local honey supplier, Hennie, and her skills with various wild creatures. I took my phone from my pocket and called, then left a message in her voicemail saying, "I need your help. We have a giant turtle and can't move it. Stop down when you finish your honey deliveries."

I then called Enid at Rollie's and explained, "I have a massive turtle in my driveway, and I'm not sure what to do about it."

"Well, dear, I can tell you, they are stubborn things. I couldn't get rid of old Speedy once he showed up. That diaper is the only concession I could get him to make."

"You didn't bring the turtle to the store?"

She laughed. "Goodness, no. He just got in one day and refused to leave. Pooped all over and made a dreadful mess. I was so glad when the diaper worked out. Though, it's not fun changing him. Worse than a baby."

I wrinkled my nose in disgust. "Do you think the turtle on my road will move on her own?"

"Well, she has to eat sometime, doesn't she?"

"Right." I sighed. "I guess I can put up a sign or something until she moves so she doesn't get run over. Thanks, Enid."

"Anytime, Thea. You and that cute boyfriend of yours stop by and see me soon."

"I told you, he's not my boyfriend. We're just keeping things casual."

"Sure, dear. Bye, bye now."

When I ended the call, I checked online to see how often alligator snapping turtles ate. Once every other day. Hopefully it'd been a while since her last meal.

Nolan was quiet most of the day, which still frustrated me. I didn't have time to do much about it because I was deep into Fourth of July planning. So many little things left to order or confirm: food, drinks, games, contests, crowd control. Every element needed to be perfect. And I still had to come in under budget somehow. The afternoon flew by without me taking a break from planning.

When Sally stuck her head in my office to say goodbye for the day, I rubbed my eyes and looked at the clock.

"Guess it's a good time for me to quit, too," I said.

Sally scrunched her face and played with her fingers. "Could I ask one little teensy favor?"

"Sure. What's up?"

"Well, if you could just not mention the turtle? Or not advertise it anywhere?"

I raised an eyebrow. "I hope she's gone when I walk outside. I don't want her sticking around, either. I thought your boys would be excited, though."

"Well, that's the thing. I've been thinking about it, and if they know there's a turtle here, they'll want to come with me to work to see it. And then they'll see the puppy and the kittens and remember the pool and the playground, and they won't ever want to leave. And I just... can't have that. They'll be running crazy while I'm trying to work and have a little quiet." She laughed nervously.

I thought for a moment, then got an idea. "The thing is, I can't really have kids running around while you're working, so you just tell them that your boss is mean and won't let them come with you."

Her face lit up. "That's perfect! Thank you!" She hugged her purse tight to her chest. "Maybe I can take some photos and that will be good enough."

"And hopefully the turtle will be long gone by the Fourth."

"Oh, right." Sally's face fell. "They'll be here for that, won't they?"

"That doesn't change the fact that you're not allowed to have them here while you're working." I made a fake stern face.

She nodded once, hard. "Right. That's all I have to say. Mommy's not allowed, and that's that." The grin returned, and she waved her fingers before walking out of sight.

Hearing stories about her four-year-old twin boys made me feel a rare moment of relief that I didn't have any kids of my own. Sally seemed to enjoy her job as registration person mostly because it got her out of the house and away from the chaos of her home life.

I stood to stretch and walked outside into the evening light. To my great relief, no turtle sat on the driveway. I moved the Stop sign back into its proper place in front of the gate.

I called to Nolan on the walkie, "I'm done for the night. Do you have my dog?"

"Yes. I also have burgers ready to grill. Want to eat?"

My late lunch had been rushed and was hours ago. "Be right there."

I walked past several occupied tent sites on my way to the seasonal section, where Nolan's site was. Many campers were cooking over fires, enjoying a quiet evening. I waved as I walked by, grateful for each one of them.

I reached Curtis's site, and his camper was bright inside with music pouring through the walls. For a moment, Curtis and his girlfriend, Rose, were visible through the window. Curtis held her close, and they danced in a slow, stiff shuffle. I smiled and chuckled to myself. Ever since Curtis had laid eyes on the widowed cornhole champion last month, he'd been smitten. And I suspected Rose was the reason Curtis continued to wear his decades-old Navy uniform to work, though it wasn't a requirement for his job surveilling the campground. It was nice to think that even at 82, love could be found.

When I neared Nolan's site, the farthest back from the rest of the campground, the smell of charcoal and cooking meat wafted from behind his camper. He'd built a small deck out back so he could sit facing the woods. I circled the camper, and Gar bounded over to me, licking my hand in greeting.

"Smells good," I said.

Nolan stood behind the grill, arms crossed, watching the burgers sizzle. I barely received a glance and a head nod for a hello.

I sat in one of his padded folding chairs and leaned back, looking up into the darkening sky as the stars blinked into view. Crickets sang as the grill popped and hissed. I took in several long breaths and tried to figure out what I failed to see in the situation. What bothered Nolan so deeply?

By the time the burgers were ready, he still hadn't said a word. He handed me a plate and sat in the chair beside mine, then stuffed his burger into his mouth. I did the same. He wouldn't be much good for talking while he ate, anyhow.

We finished the burgers—one for me, three for him—and he sat up in his chair, tapping his fingertips together.

"What are you waiting for?" My voice sounded thunderous as it broke the silent tension between us.

"What do you mean?" He didn't look at me.

"There's obviously something going on with you, but you haven't said what."

He growled and rubbed his forehead.

I watched him for several long minutes. "Nolan, please."

He huffed. "Look. If there will be fireworks on the Fourth, I can't be here."

"I don't get it. What's the big deal?"

"It's not so much the fireworks themselves as the sounds they make."

I considered his words, but things weren't adding up. "Do you have sensitive ears?"

He shook his head. "You know it's common for soldiers to get PTSD, right?"

"I don't see how you couldn't."

He shrugged. "Some things are more common triggers than others."

"And the fireworks... remind you of war?"

"They sound like gunfire and bombs. It's worse when it's unexpected. So, if you're going to allow campers to set them off, even those little snapping ones..."

I hadn't considered something like that. I suffered from PTSD myself, so I understood how triggers worked, but mine were very different from what Nolan experienced. Loud, sudden noises rarely bothered me.

"I'm sorry. I didn't realize," I said. "We don't have to allow campers to have them. That sounds dangerous, anyhow."

"I usually retreat into the woods for several days this time of year to escape it. Don't know what I'll do this year."

"I didn't mean to create a difficult situation for you."

"It's fine. I'll figure something out. But you might need extra security if I have to be gone."

"Sure." I nodded. "I certainly won't make you stay somewhere that might upset you or make you feel unsafe."

He looked at me sideways. "Don't do that."

"What am I doing?"

"Acting like I'm some kind of pansy for not wanting to be around fireworks."

"I didn't say anything like that," I snapped.

He rubbed the back of his neck and chugged a beer that had been sitting by his foot. He crumpled the can and threw it across the deck. "People who haven't been there don't understand. It's not like I'm *afraid* of loud noises."

I pulled in a slow breath and tried to decide how to respond. His anger spiked my anxiety. "Nolan, you're the toughest, strongest, manliest man I've ever known. I doubt you're afraid of anything. But I can understand a little. I mean, when goofing around almost gives you a panic attack, it's not much fun, either."

It had been a day not long after I hired Nolan that we'd been playing around with the hose and he'd grabbed me in a bear hug. It still made my heart pound to think of the feeling of being held against my will, unable to break free. I reached over and put my hand on his.

"If I thought you were any kind of pansy," I continued, "I wouldn't pay you to do security, and I definitely wouldn't call you every time something scary happens."

After several minutes, he turned to me. "Want to go for a walk?"

I nodded and stood. He held my hand as we circled around the looping roads of the campground with Gar in tow. Nolan didn't say much and neither did I. The few times I'd seen him rattled by something, he tended to be quiet. Lost in his own thoughts, hopefully not beating himself up too much.

We strolled along every road, not in any hurry. By the time we ended up near the path to my cabin, it had been an hour. The kittens ran in front of us as we turned down the trail. Three sets of black paw prints dotted the path. "I can only imagine what those three get up to all day."

Nolan walked me to my door and gave me a long kiss goodnight. The relief from his affection melted over me and filled my chest with warmth. He squeezed my hands before turning away.

"Hey," I said.

He paused and looked over his shoulder.

"Don't stress over this."

He nodded and walked off.

I let Gar inside and poured food into his bowl. While he chomped it down, I leaned my elbows on the kitchen counter and thought through what Nolan had said and not said.

How many others were like him, dreading this holiday? What if somehow I could make Cedar Fish safe for Nolan, but also for anyone who might want to escape the noise and still enjoy the Fourth? Nolan never talked about being a soldier or the aftereffects of it. I wished I knew more about his time in the military and as a cop and what things still haunted him from those days. I also still didn't know why he'd been fired from the force, and anytime I asked, he changed the subject. Something deep in my soul worried it might be so bad that if I knew, I'd change my mind about him.

I considered Nolan's pained expression, his hesitation at even admitting something was bothering him. My chest ached for him. There was only one thing to do. I'd have to cancel the fireworks display. The deposit money would be gone, but I'd get back my first payment, according to the contract. The idea of losing that money sat like a rock in my stomach, but what choice did I have? I just hoped I had time to rebrand the event and bring in enough reservations to make up for the money I'd lose on the fireworks.

Get it here:

ZoeyChase.com/OneBodyShortOfAPicnic

About the Author

Zoey Chase received her MFA in creative writing from Carlow University. She lives in the Pittsburgh area with her husband, three daughters, three cats, and vast book collection. Can usually be found doing something bookish.

www.ZoeyChase.com
Facebook: /AuthorZoeyChase
Instagram: @AuthorZoeyChase